THE WRLD BANK and the ENVIRONMENT

First Annual Report
Fiscal 1990

The World Bank
Washington, D.C.

This publication was prepared by World Bank staff, and the findings, interpretations, and conclusions expressed in it do not necessarily represent the views of the Bank's Board of Executive Directors or the countries they represent. The World Bank does not guarantee the accuracy of the data included in this publication and accepts no responsibility whatsoever for any consequences of their use.

The text is printed on recycled paper that exceeds the requirements of the 1988 guidelines of the U.S. Environmental Protection Agency, section 6002 of the Resource Conservation and Recovery Act. The paper stock contains at least 50 percent recovered waste paper material as calculated by fiber content, of which at least 10 percent of the total fiber is postconsumer waste and 20 to 50 percent of the fiber has been deinked.

ISSN 1014-8132
ISBN 0-8213-1641-9

Contents

This report was prepared by Jeremy J. Warford and Zeinab Partow, both of the Environment Department of the World Bank. Significant comments and contributions were made by staff throughout the Bank and the International Finance Corporation.

Overview

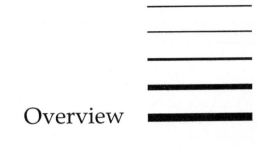

That environmental degradation in its many forms constitutes a significant threat to economic development has become evident during the past decade. Sound environmental management has been recognized as fundamental to the development process, and the World Bank now emphasizes the need to make environmental concerns an integral part of its activities.

Although considerable progress has recently been made in this direction, a Bank report to the Development Committee in September 1989 set out a three-year agenda for action that called for greater efforts in a number of areas. It recommended that actions be taken to bring environmental strategy into the mainstream of country economic work, to strengthen research on the underlying causes of environmental degradation and on the feasibility of appropriate policy interventions, to implement a new environmental assessment methodology, to increase lending for free-standing environmental and population projects, to expand its efforts in staff training and guidance of Bank staff on environmental matters, and to participate more effectively in the international environmental debate.

Major environmental concerns were addressed in Bank operations in fiscal 1990 through country-focused environmental strategy work, policy and research activities, and lending operations. Five problem areas require special attention from the Bank and its members:

- Destruction of natural habitats
- Land degradation
- Degradation and depletion of fresh water resources
- Urban, industrial, and agricultural pollution
- Degradation of the "global commons."[1]

---

1. The use of this term does not necessarily imply recognition of international legal obligations regarding such "commons" in the absence of treaty provisions to this effect.

1

Environmental Strategy

Developing environmental strategies for specific countries involves efforts to identify environmental issues of special concern, to search for direct and underlying causes of those problems, to identify policy interventions and general investment needs, and to identify the appropriate form and sources of external assistance. Major environmental strategy work in developing countries has been the product of a cooperative process between the country concerned, the Bank, and other intergovernmental or bilateral development agencies. When appropriate, relevant nongovernmental organizations (NGOs) are involved in this process.

Country environmental strategies take many forms. They may be countrywide or directed at more localized problems. They may be free-standing exercises or may form a part of macroeconomic work or lending operations; they may also be conducted on a regional basis. All of these approaches were used during the past year. The Bank helped several African countries to complete comprehensive, countrywide action plans. Specific topics, such as industrial pollution, were covered in the lending operations in other countries, such as China, Indonesia, and Poland. Integrated natural resource management, initially studied as part of agriculture sector work for the Philippines, is the subject of a proposed environmental sector loan, and the Environmental Program for the Mediterranean (EPM) is a major regional initiative.

The Bank's studies to date highlight both the importance and the difficulty of establishing cause and effect relationships in environmental problems. They point to the appropriate policies and investments needed to correct existing problems or to prevent further ones from occurring. The range of factors that lead, directly or indirectly, to environmental problems often includes poverty, rapid population growth, insecurity of land tenure, economic incentives that encourage unsustainable use of resources, and inadequate legal framework or institutional capacity.

These studies also stress the importance of policies designed to foster in developing countries a pattern of growth that is more efficient and less resource-intensive than that which has characterized development in the industrial countries. Fortunately, opportunities do exist for policies and investments in which economic and environmental objectives coincide, such as pricing energy at its true economic cost.

Recent experience suggests that environmental action plans can be implemented as distinct activities leading to investment programs, policy and institutional reform, and coordination of donor effort, as in Madagascar and Mauritius. Significant progress in implementing environmental measures will also be achieved through addressing specific environmental problems that are inherent in routine operational activities, such as country economic and sector work. This is clearly consistent with the objective of making environmental concerns integral to Bank operations. Sector work of this kind has formed a solid base for environmental lending in fiscal 1990 in Brazil, Côte d'Ivoire, Madagascar, and Poland. Such work will also influence an increasing number of environmental loans in years to come.

Policy and Research

A wide range of policy and research activities was undertaken during the year. Work on natural habitats placed considerable emphasis on preservation of biodiversity. The Bank has collaborated with leading environmental NGOs in a variety of activities in this field, including the publication of a new book, *Conserving the World's Biological Diversity*. A major initiative begun during the year was preparation of a new forestry policy paper. The paper will provide Bank staff and country personnel with guidelines for effective forest management, especially as it relates to curbing deforestation and the loss of natural habitat. The Bank has also reviewed its performance on large dams and has recommended future actions related to the environmental aspects of dams and the special issue of dam safety. Dam construction often involves the involuntary resettlement of local populations, and a new staff directive on this topic contains guidelines on how to avoid or ameliorate resettlement problems.

Work on land degradation during the year revolved primarily around farm policies and incentives, technological constraints, land tenure issues, and community participation. A series of activities on drylands was carried out, and papers were published on techniques for measuring dryland degradation and on the lessons of experience in drylands management. Other work sought to identify the critical variables in soil management; the use of vetiver grass on contours to improve soil and moisture conservation to counter soil erosion; and issues in social forestry. The economic consequences of land degradation is a key topic in the Bank's long-term perspective study, *Sub-Saharan Africa: From Crisis to Sustainable Growth*, which recognizes that land degradation has a direct bearing on agriculture, food security, and energy production in the region and thus integrates environmental issues into its basic analysis of economic and social conditions in Africa.

The degradation and depletion of fresh water resources is posing increasing threats to economic development in many countries. An effort to replace traditional sectoral strategies with an integrated approach to water resource management—involving agricultural, energy, industrial, and municipal uses—was initiated during the year in the Asia and the Europe,

Middle East, and North Africa regions. Research projects to identify optimal investment strategies for irrigation and agricultural development, and to address the problems of waterlogging and salinity that often result from irrigation schemes, were initiated.

Rapidly growing urban populations and industrialization are leading to massive pollution problems in many countries. Air quality management is a subject of rapidly growing concern. Diagnostic studies of air pollution in Ankara and Mexico City were begun, a review of air pollution in Beijing was completed, and other studies on health effects of air pollution, pollution control strategies, and the contribution of transportation to air pollution were carried out. Issues related to agricultural pollution were also the subject of several research and policy activities, which included a review of the experience of integrated pest management in African agriculture. The Bank, assisted by a panel of external advisers, also made progress in revising its pesticide guidelines.

Various aspects of the "global commons" problem were addressed in policy and research work during the year. A collaborative effort involving several departments and led by the Bank's principal science and technology advisor resulted in the publication of *The Greenhouse Effect: Implications for Economic Development*. The paper presents a scientific perspective on the issue of global climatic change and establishes a framework for a response to the implications of global warming for natural resource conservation and economic development. Work in progress includes a paper on the effect of the production and use of chlorofluorocarbons (CFCs) on global climate and the ozone layer.

The need to integrate environmental concerns into the mainstream of country economic policy was reflected in a number of policy and research activities that cut across several topics or sectors. The book, *Environmental Management and Economic Development*, includes methodologies and case studies on natural resource management in developing countries. The potential for incorporating environmental concerns more systematically into conventional national income accounting procedures was another area under investigation, and an environmental and natural resource accounting study in Mexico was initiated. Research continued during the year on the effect of trade liberalization on the sustainability of agriculture, on incentives for smallholder tree-planting, and on the use of geographic information systems in economic planning. The policy and research work of the Energy Sector Management Assistance Program (ESMAP) continued its heavy environmental orientation, especially regarding policies aimed at energy efficiency and conservation. Research on fiscal policy and environmental management, with particular attention to the potential role of taxes on environmentally harmful activities in developing countries was also begun.

The question as to whether economic policy reform will be sufficient in the long term is of central concern to the development community. Population growth and long-run resource constraints, for example, may compromise economic growth; these issues were the subject of study. Finally, institutional constraints—broadly defined to include cultural, regulatory, and organizational factors—and their relation to a variety of aspects of the environmental problem were also themes in on-going research during the year.

Environmental Lending Operations

Lending for projects that specifically address the environment has increased. During fiscal 1990, 11 free-standing environmental loans or credits were approved, compared with 2 in the previous year. The loans are concentrated in Africa and focus on conserving natural habitats and tropical forests. Such projects are inherently complex and require major borrower and staff effort in design and implementation. In many cases staff have had to grapple with difficulties posed by the existence of significant tradeoffs between environmental and short-term economic objectives. The projects involve complex institutional arrangements, cultural and social concerns, and the perennial issue of valuation of the services provided by natural resources such as tropical forests.

Some of the free-standing environmental projects cover a range of multisectoral issues. This is the case in Brazil's national environment project, which is designed to support the first three-year phase of the country's national environmental program and in which institutional strengthening is a key objective. The Environment I Project in Madagascar also takes a comprehensive approach to environmental problems in the country, comprising components for protecting and managing biodiversity, soil conservation, watershed management, agroforestry, reforestation, institutional support, land titling, marine and coastal ecosystems research, and the establishment of a geographic information system in especially vulnerable areas. Flood protection and the related problem of wastewater disposal are the focus of another project in Madagascar, while the Abidjan Lagoon Environmental Protection Project in Côte d'Ivoire provides for construction of wastewater disposal facilities, monitoring of pollution, and establishment of sound environmental legislation. Widespread problems of environmental degradation in Poland are addressed in a project that provides a framework for developing appropriate economic and institutional policies to address the country's severe air and water pollution.

Lending for population activities is a central feature of the Bank's multi-sectoral approach to environment, and its increase was an important item on the Bank's environmental agenda. In fiscal 1990 lending for population, health, and nutrition (PHN) projects amounted to just over $800 million, of which some 20 to 25 percent was devoted to family planning. This is in line with the sector's three-year lending target set by the Bank's president in November 1989.

During fiscal 1990 the Bank continued to increase its efforts to build environmental objectives and ameliorative components into its projects. About 50 percent of Bank loans and credits during the year contained environmental components. In the agriculture sector all forestry projects now contain a strong environmental orientation. Other agricultural projects contain such elements as soil conservation; improved land use patterns, agroecological zoning, and titling; flood control and drainage; improved irrigation efficiency; integrated pest management; and rangeland and wildlife management.

Environmental issues in the industry sector have been accorded increasing attention within Bank projects. Project components range from facilities for treating effluents and installations to reduce emissions of air pollutants, to the elaboration of full-fledged strategies to control industrial pollution. Transport projects have included components for traffic management, measures to control vehicle emissions and to mitigate pollution in ports, and criteria for road design that avoid environmental damage to forests and agricultural land. Water supply projects now invariably involve measures to dispose of wastewater safely and efficiently, and urbanization projects contain a variety of environmental components, including improvements in overall regulatory capacity, drainage, solid waste management, and sanitation.

Energy development raises many issues of environmental concern—threats to human and natural habitats posed by hydro projects; unsustainable use of renewable and nonrenewable fuels; water and air pollution; and emissions of greenhouse gases. Energy efficiency measures, including pricing policies and the search for least-cost solutions are standard elements of energy lending. These procedures are supported by preinvestment and other country-based activities completed or under way in the ESMAP program, which during fiscal 1990 continued to include numerous studies of household energy use with heavy emphasis on improving the efficient production and use of biomass-based energy.

Adjustment lending has begun to consciously incorporate measures to protect or enhance the management of natural resources. In fiscal 1990 resource degradation in the agricultural and forestry sector were addressed through institutional and economic reforms in loans to the Central African

Republic, Côte d'Ivoire, Ghana, Guyana, Mali, Mauritania, and Uganda. In addition to adjustment lending specifically oriented toward environment, a number of adjustment programs included conditions likely to—as a by-product—benefit the environment. Typical components in such projects during fiscal 1990 have included the elimination or reduction of subsidies for pesticides, full-cost recovery in pricing energy or water services, and improved land distribution policies and tenure arrangements.

An important development in the Bank's efforts to incorporate environmental considerations into its lending activities was the introduction of the Operational Directive on Environmental Assessment. This directive is meant to ensure that development options are environmentally sound and sustainable and that any environmental consequences are recognized early in the project cycle and taken into account in project design. It also provides a formal mechanism to address a range of issues, including the concerns of affected local groups and relevant NGOs. Implementation of the directive is now well under way. Training programs for Bank staff and for developing-country officials were initiated during the year. The Bank's *Monthly Operational Summary* will now provide more detailed information on the categorization of projects according to their expected environmental impact as well as on important environmental issues that may arise and on the actions proposed to address them.

The supervision of several projects approved in earlier years, some of which have been controversial, has commanded considerable staff effort during the past year. Such projects include the National Land Management and Livestock Project in Botswana; the Sardar Sarovar Dam in India; the Singrauli Thermal Power Project, also in India; the Kedung Ombo project in Indonesia: the Carajas Iron Ore project in Brazil; and the Northwest III Settlement Project (Polonoroeste) in Brazil. This supervision has been concerned with measures to protect the environment and to mitigate the potential adverse effects of certain investments on local populations.

Although growing concern with the environmental aspects of projects— as exemplified by the introduction of a more systematic environmental assessment process—should reduce such problems in the future, project monitoring is likely, on balance, to require much greater attention than in the past. The growing number of free-standing environmental projects and environmental components that involve heavy inputs from Bank staff in the identification and preparation process will have to be matched by a substantial increase in monitoring and supervision efforts—by both the Bank and its borrowers.

Special Funding Arrangements

Global environmental problems, such as the threat to the ozone layer, the greenhouse effect, the loss of biodiversity, and ocean pollution reflect the growing physical and economic interdependence among nations. Although primary responsibility for global environmental problems continues to rest with the industrial countries, developing countries will contribute increasingly to global air and water pollution as their economies expand. A central concern in addressing global issues continues to be the question of how best to assist developing countries in taking measures to protect the "global commons." Additional concessionary funding will be required where the country bears the costs for environmental protection, but where the benefits accrue to the global community. To facilitate additional and concessional funding of global environmental actions by developing countries in the four areas listed above, the Bank has been consulting with both donor and borrower countries to establish a Global Environmental Facility. This initiative would be undertaken in cooperation with United Nations Environment Programme (UNEP) and the United Nations Development Programme (UNDP) and would provide funding for programs in these areas.

A related example, which could be a prototype for international cooperation on matters of common concern, is the agreement reached by the parties to the Montreal Protocol to establish a special fund of at least $160 million over three years to protect the ozone layer. The Bank has been asked to administer and manage this fund, which will finance the incremental costs incurred by developing countries in addressing global environmental concerns.

An additional way to transfer resources to developing countries to improve the environment is through debt-for-nature swaps. NGOs have helped to arrange 10 debt-for-nature transactions in 7 countries, including Bolivia, Costa Rica, Ecuador, Madagascar, the Philippines, Poland, and Zambia. Although the Bank does not participate directly in financing such transactions, it is prepared to facilitate the process.

Implementation of environmental projects has often been constrained by inadequate funds for project preparation. Recognizing this, several bilateral donors have recently provided additional grant funds for technical assistance. In mid-1989 the Bank set up a Technical Assistance Grant Program for the Environment, based largely on a grant of $16.6 million from Japan.

The World Bank and the International Community

The Bank's links with the international community take several forms, including formal and informal meetings with other international agencies and bilateral aid donors, links with leading environmental NGOs, and the many special events that have an environmental theme. The Bank's activities in these areas include symposiums on key resources such as energy and water; gatherings of scientists, consulting engineers, officials, and parliamentarians; and more specialized groupings—for environmental economists, experts on natural disasters, and advisers on industrial risk management—that the Bank itself has convened or sponsored. Senior managers participated in the conference on Global Environment and Human Response towards Sustainable Development in Tokyo and in the European and North American Ministers' Conference in Bergen, Norway, on Action for a Common Future. A very important future event will be the 1992 UN Conference on Environment and Development. The publication of the Bank's *World Development Report 1992*—which will have the environment as its principal theme—will coincide with the conference.

Progress and Prospects

The Bank has made considerable progress during the past fiscal year in responding to the agenda set out in the September 1989 report to the Development Committee. Lending targets in the environmental and population sectors are being achieved, and implementation of the environmental assessment procedure is well under way. Considerable advances were made during the year in international environmental activities, and the Bank has played its part in these developments. The Bank has made good progress in building matters of environmental concern into country economic work, but much remains to be done. To this end, much applied research on the feasibility of various policy interventions is required, as is a continuing emphasis on staff training. For the future, plans must be made to anticipate the demands on staff and borrowers if proper implementation of environmental components of projects and policies is to be achieved.

A key question for the longer term is how to reconcile sound environmental activities with economic growth. Economic growth has traditionally been linked with depletion of the earth's natural resources and is now placing growing pressure on the earth's assimilative capacity. Progress in the transition to sustainable rates of population growth will serve both environmental and developmental objectives. Prospects for future economic development may be enhanced as well through technical progress in the efficient use of resources and through the design of policies that foster a pattern of economic growth that is less resource-intensive. The Bank will continue to help developing countries respond to these challenges. Industrial countries can contribute to this effort in a variety of ways—through concessional aid, reform of their own domestic policies and practices, and scientific and technical research.

1. Development of an Environmental Awareness

The World Bank recruited its first environmental adviser in 1969 and established an Office of Environmental Affairs shortly thereafter. The Bank has played an active role in this area, and by the mid-1980s it had financed numerous projects containing environmental components as well as several free-standing environmental projects, which had solely environmental objectives, such as reforestation, watershed management, and pollution control.

During the past decade or so, there has been growing evidence that environmental degradation in its many forms constitutes a threat of growing significance to economic development. In addition the rapid evolution of the environmental agenda has led to an increased understanding of the interdependence among economic activities and their environmental consequences, both within and between countries. The economic and physical interdependence between nations is illustrated by the emergence of new kinds of environmental problems, such as the deterioration of the ozone layer, the greenhouse effect, tropical deforestation, and the transboundary movement of hazardous wastes.

It became apparent that the Bank's response did not match the changing realities either in the degree of effort devoted to environmental matters or in the approaches actually used. This, combined with a few well-publicized cases in which Bank projects actually had negative environmental consequences—such as contributing to the destruction of tropical rain forests and posing threats to wildlife, indigenous people, and established human settlements—prompted the institution to rethink and adjust its policies toward environmental management. In particular, Bank management decided to bring environmental concerns more systematically into the mainstream of its operations.

International recognition of the economic importance of environmental degradation was evidenced by the decision of the Development Committee, which is comprised of finance ministers from both developing and industrial countries, to discuss the subject in May 1987. A report to the committee, prepared by Bank staff, was an important step in setting out the general principles that have subsequently governed the institution's overall approach to the environment. Drawing on lessons from Bank experience, the report recognized that environmental issues were becoming increasingly important in macroeconomic terms. It also emphasized that because of the pervasive nature of environmental problems, the traditional project-by-project approach had to be supplemented by integrating environmental management into economic policymaking at all levels of government. It concluded that special attention should be given to designing economic incentives to induce environmentally sound behavior and provided examples of economic policies that satisfied both economic and environmental objectives and that also, in most cases, contributed to alleviating poverty.

One year later the Bank again reported to the Development Committee. This time it described the measures it had taken to implement the recommended principles as well as the changes resulting from the overall reorganization of the Bank in July 1987. These changes included the creation of a central Environment Department and four regional environmental divisions and an increase in the number of environmental staff. Various procedures designed to integrate environmental considerations into the Bank's work were also introduced.

Since it is now recognized that sound environmental management is fundamental to the development process, the Bank's new policy emphasizes the need to make environmental issues an integral part of all its activities. In practice, environmental considerations are now being addressed through a continuum of activities that range from a series of country studies of environmental strategy—including country environmental action plans and regional studies—to country economic and sector work, project and adjustment lending, and evaluation.

An Agenda for Action

Progress in integrating environmental concerns throughout the Bank's operations was described more fully in yet a third report to the Development Committee for its September 1989 meeting. This report concluded that, although considerable progress had been made in integrating environmental concerns into the Bank's operations, in certain areas improvement needed to be hastened and other actions taken to maintain the momentum that had been built up. The following agenda for action was proposed for the next three years:

- Increase the emphasis on environmental concerns in country economic work; this will include analyzing the implications of environmental degradation for sustainable economic development and recommending economic policies to improve environmental management.

- Strengthen research on the underlying causes of environmental degradation; the relations between population, poverty, and the environment; and the feasibility of appropriate policy interventions.
- Work closely with borrowers to use the environmental assessment methodology systematically in preparing and evaluating projects to be financed by the Bank.
- Increase lending for free-standing environmental projects.
- Increase lending for population projects.
- Develop a permanent program to train operational staff—especially country economists and task managers—on the environmental aspects of their work.
- Expand staff guidelines on several key issues; this will include updating environmental guidelines for industry and preparing guidelines on land and water management.
- Continue to be involved in international efforts to develop policies on emerging environmental topics, such as the "global commons" issues.
- Improve and increase the flow of environmental information outside the Bank by making this an integral part of the Bank's public awareness and education strategy.

Priority Environmental Problems

This ambitious agenda calls for a Bank-wide effort to bring environmental issues into the mainstream of lending operations and policy work. Evidence from the Bank's experience and from its environmental issues papers and other background work has identified five priority environmental problems that require special attention by the Bank and its member countries: destruction of natural habitats; land degradation; degradation and depletion of fresh water resources; urban, industrial, and agricultural pollution; and degradation of the "global commons." These five problems have been addressed in Bank operations through various country-focused environmental action plans, through coverage of environmental issues in country economic and sector work, and through actual lending operations, consisting of both free-standing environmental projects and environmental components of other projects as well as adjustment lending.

Because of the complex interactions among the many underlying causes of such environmental problems, increased attention is needed—in operational as well as policy and research work—to the effects of population growth, policy and market failures, and legal, institutional and management shortcomings, as well as the special financing needs created by environmental degradation.

This first annual report responds to the request made by the Development Committee in 1988, in which it called on the Bank's Executive Board to review and publish an annual report on the environmental aspects of its operations; this report would include an assessment of selected projects having major environmental impact. The following chapters describe progress made by the Bank in fiscal 1990 in pursuing the agenda listed above— with special reference to the five priority problems—and recommend areas for future work. The report primarily addresses the role of the Bank as it relates to environmental management within developing countries. However, there are limits to what the developing countries and development assistance agencies can accomplish alone. Although much can be done to improve environmental management in developing countries, the policies of industrial nations are critical to sound environmental management in many areas; for example, the industrial countries are primarily responsible for some of the major global impacts, such as carbon dioxide emissions.

2. Environmental Strategy

The nature and significance of environmental problems obviously varies tremendously from country to country, but in the most general terms, the priority environmental issues facing the developing world fall into the five categories identified in chapter 1: destruction of natural habitats; land degradation; degradation and depletion of fresh water resources; urban, industrial, and agricultural pollution; and degradation of the "global commons."

These priority environmental problems are translated into operational strategies in the Bank through a series of activities conducted in close cooperation with borrowers. These include environmental lending strategies, various forms of country action plans, and regional activities. Before fiscal 1990 the Bank devoted considerable effort to developing strategies to deal with major environmental problems on a country-by-country basis. Environmental issues papers now have been completed for virtually all borrowing countries. These internal documents have heightened awareness of environmental concerns among Bank staff and have clarified responsibility for environmental matters in Bank country operations. Overall the process has increased the consistency with which environmental issues are addressed in the individual countries.

The environmental issues papers are the first step in a continuum of activities that may ultimately lead to policy reform or environmental investments. The papers provide the background for more in-depth analysis of priority environmental problems in many countries, so that overall strategies for dealing with them can be developed. In practice such analysis involves four steps:

- Identify priority problems
- Search for direct and underlying causes of those problems
- Identify policy interventions and general investment needs
- Identify the appropriate form and sources of external assistance.

Exercises of this kind, conducted by Bank staff or consultants in partnership with the countries concerned, can lead to the adoption of country environmental strategies.

Country Environmental Strategies

In assisting governments to develop environmental strategies, the Bank's work must always be built on the environmental profiles, strategy documents, and sectoral and economic analyses that have been done by the countries themselves, as well as by other international and bilateral agencies. The work must also take into account relevant work done by nongovernmental organizations (NGOs). In view of the large number of such studies the Bank's role is often to draw together and synthesize existing material and to give it an operational focus, with special attention to introducing opportunities for policy reform and new investment. Environmental strategy work in developing countries has involved close cooperation among the concerned governments, the Bank, other development agencies, and relevant NGOs.

In Africa comprehensive, countrywide environmental action plans have now been completed by a number of countries. In addition to those previously done by Lesotho, Madagascar, and Mauritius, action plans were substantially completed by Ghana and Rwanda during this fiscal year, and work is in progress in Burkina Faso, Burundi, Guinea, and Tunisia. Where more detailed analysis is required or when larger countries are concerned, environmental strategy work focuses on specific problems. The strategy studies may be incorporated into sector or economic work, or they may address a specific problem, such as air or water pollution, deforestation, or flood mitigation (Box 2-1).

Where environmental concerns cannot be effectively addressed by individual countries, regional studies are often required. Such an approach is useful when several countries experience similar problems and where valuable lessons can be learned through multicountry analysis. Most of the studies—and certainly all of the countrywide environmental action plans—have been developed with the participation of the larger donor community and focus on identifying specific investments and policy prescriptions to address the five priority environmental problems already listed. The types of action promoted by the Bank can be summarized under each heading.

• Destruction of Natural Habitats. This issue encompasses a wide range of problems that have a direct effect on the viability of natural ecosystems, including the loss of diversity in animal and plant species in terrestrial and aquatic ecosystems and the destruction of areas of scenic

---

Box 2–1. Flood Mitigation in Bangladesh

The severe floods of 1987 and 1988 stimulated considerable international interest in helping Bangladesh to mitigate the environmental and social effects of floods. Initially this took the form of studies—carried out by the United Nations Development Programme (UNDP), France, Japan, and the United States—to evaluate the problem and recommend solutions. All the reports pointed to the need for careful investigation and planning before any major investments were made. However, they differed in their vision of the outcome of such studies. Some reports basically advocated "living with the flood," while others envisaged an extensive complex of embankments and drainage pumps.

Having agreed to help Bangladesh coordinate this international effort, in July 1989 the Bank brought together the various Bangladeshi and international experts who had worked on the recent studies. The group decided to prepare a short-term plan concentrating on priority projects as well as studies designed to give a better understanding of the problems of flood control and drainage in specific areas.

A program of regional and supporting studies, now in progress, forms a central feature of the plan. Efforts will be made to devise measures to reduce the environmental and social impact of floods without creating adverse effects. The flood and drainage problems and potentials of each region will be identified by the regional studies carried out in parallel with supporting work focussing on special topics, such as fisheries, wildlife, aquatic ecology, the response of farmers to floods, experience with existing flood control and drainage works, and a general overview of flood-related environmental issues.

---

beauty. Natural habitats are threatened primarily by indiscriminate land clearing and development of forests, wildlands, and wetlands; pollution; illegal capture and trade in endangered species; and overexploitation through hunting. In addition many of the factors leading to the destruction of natural habitats also hurt vulnerable population groups, including tribal peoples and other communities who rely on minimally disturbed natural ecosystems for their physical survival and cultural identity.

The environmental action plans and strategies developed or implemented during fiscal 1990 strongly emphasize measures to address the destruction of natural habitats. For example, the environmental action plan in Rwanda stresses the need to educate populations living around national parks about park management. Conservation and improved management of wetlands is another priority, and less dependence on fuelwood is encouraged to reduce both the pressure on forest resources and the level of air pollution. Protection and study of the unique and little-known ecosystem of Mount Nimba in Guinea is a focus of that country's action plan, and the protection of Madagascar's remaining rainforests and its many endemic species has proven a highly motivating objective for that country and its donors. Within its overall program to strengthen environmental management and protection, Brazil plans to strengthen the national system of conservation units and to develop regional action plans for critically endangered ecosystems. The action plan in Tunisia also gives prominence to protecting unique wetland ecosystems, such as Lake Ichkeul.

A review of Papua New Guinea's tropical forestry action plan identifies significant problems in the forestry sector and specifies priorities for action (see Box 2-4, below). One basic problem is the lack of adequate information for assessing the status of forest resources and formulating policies for sustainable development. As a first step the study proposes a complete inventory of forestry resources. To remedy weak administration and management of forest resources, other proposed actions include the creation of a national forestry board to formulate national forestry policies and plans; standing committees to assist the board in such areas as conservation, land use, research, and marketing; and regional forestry boards to administer forest development plans and issue timber licenses. Recommendations on forest conservation and land use include formulation of a national conservation strategy with participation of community, government, and industry interests; programs to rehabilitate national parks, to improve ecological survey and monitoring, and to train local leaders in land use management; and a feasibility study for establishing a land use research council.

• Land Degradation. Land degradation includes sheet and gully erosion, soil compaction, waterlogging and salinization, and nutrient depletion—all of which reduce soil productivity. This, in turn, has deleterious effects both on and off the farm. Deforestation is also significant not only because of its threat to natural habitats, as described above, but also because it is perhaps the most serious cause of land degradation in developing countries and, at the same time, an important factor in global issues such as biodiversity and climate change. The many causes of deforestation include commercial logging, conversion of forest lands to urban and agricultural uses, and unsustainable exploitation of land for activities such as cattle ranching. Pasture and rangeland degradation, along with soil erosion and deforestation, is occurring in many regions as human and livestock pressures approach or exceed the carrying capacities of the rangelands. In fact all aspects of land degradation are being exacerbated by increased population pressures, combined with ambiguous property rights, the breakdown of traditional land management regimes, and external shocks such as prolonged drought.

Various forms of land degradation pose some of the most serious problems facing developing countries around the world, as highlighted by environmental strategy work conducted in certain countries. Burkina Faso's Village Level Land Management Program, initiated before the action plan, will help the country encourage better land use practices, including soil conservation, water harvesting, forest and wildlife management and protection, and improved livestock management. The economic importance of environmental problems is also recognized in the country economic memorandum for Burkina Faso, which includes environmental issues in a proposed adjustment strategy for the agriculture sector. Relevant areas for environmental concern include institutional mechanisms for implementing land reform, community-based land management, land use planning, and natural resource management as well as innovative programs for conserving pastureland and cultivating fodder crops.

Comprehensive policy and technical discussions are under way with federal and state officials in Nigeria on environmental programs aimed, among other things, at strengthening environmental institutions, developing technology options for better land management, and designing information systems to improve understanding of the underlying causes of past and present deterioration in vegetation cover and soil fertility.

The agriculture sector study in Algeria also places heavy emphasis on conservation and environmental matters. It recommends land policy reforms to encourage private investments in land improvements, such as creating a market in land-use rights; investments in irrigation and prevention of reservoir sedimentation; and introduction of water conservation measures, including realistic irrigation water charges and recycling wastewater for irrigation. A program to protect soils and water catchments is also proposed; this would include preparing forest management plans, defining priority areas for erosion control, strengthening the planning framework for forest resources utilization, and adjusting the price of forest products.

Ongoing work in the Philippines provides an excellent illustration of how to integrate strategic work on the problems of land and water use with that on resource degradation. The "Philippines Environment and Natural Resource Management Study" addresses the adverse effects on long-term productivity of the most significant environmental problems and outlines a comprehensive strategy for improving natural resource management through institutional and policy reform (Box 2-2).

Another significant activity completed in this fiscal year was a study on natural resource management for sustainable development in Nepal, done

20

Box 2–2. Philippines: Environment and Natural Resource Management Study

This study, published in September 1989, identifies significant environmental problems, including the degradation and disappearance of forests, which once covered nearly one half of the country; erosion and changes in hydrologic regimes as a result of converting forest to other land uses; the transformation of mangrove swamps to fishponds; the degradation of coral reefs; and the depletion of near-shore fisheries through overfishing and destructive techniques. These problems are closely linked to population and rural poverty, the use and management of common-access resources, the institutional requirements of resource management, and the pricing of resources.

The study concludes that the main thrust of government policy should be to develop an institutional and incentive structure that will encourage people to adopt sustainable resource management techniques. Such a structure would involve full extraction of economic rents by the government; restricting rights of access to public resources; increased privatization of user rights through titling with use restrictions or through improved leasehold grants on public land; and community-based projects for watershed management and agricultural development. Application of these principles on forested uplands would entail specific measures, such as delineation of protected areas (for example, parks, biological reserves, mangrove swamps, and critical watersheds) to be excluded from logging for environmental reasons; institution of a pricing system for land use or timber extraction in public areas open to commercial activities; implementation of community forestry programs; and development of a tenure system to encourage upland farmers to adopt sustainable cultivation techniques.

In the coastal zones the strategy calls for introducing common-property management systems and a more equitable access to coastal resources through enforcement of access rights. Specific measures would include legislation to grant local governments the rights to license fishing activities with restrictions imposed under national regulations, tenure instruments for the replanting or sustained use of mangrove areas, and legislation to prohibit the use of destructive fishing techniques and new conversions of mangrove swamps to fishponds. These general principles are now forming the basis for an environmental sector loan planned for fiscal 1991.

with the assistance of the British Overseas Development Administration. It examines feasible policies, institutions, and investment activities in the country, with special emphasis on the hill regions. The study analyzes the character of natural resource degradation, its direct and indirect causes, and the policies that contribute to these causes. It is intended that the study will be used by both donors and the government in shaping future programs to alleviate the negative effects of natural resource degradation on the economy.

In fiscal 1990 an analysis of tropical deforestation and the degradation of the altiplano in Bolivia was also completed. The study has helped to set the scene for an environmental action plan, in which the US Agency for International Development (USAID) will play a leading role.

• Degradation and Depletion of Fresh Water Resources. In many developing countries, overuse of both surface and ground water resources is leading to scarcity and deteriorating quality of water. In many large coastal urban areas, polluted surface water causes local people to overdraw aquifers, which in turn causes salinization, particularly of the shallow groundwater on which poor people depend. Management problems are complex, and the problems of allocating water among competing uses are becoming increasingly difficult and important as supplies diminish.

A large number of countries have made improved management of water resources a priority in their environmental action plans and strategies. Burkina Faso and Ghana focus on the critical importance of adequate water supplies in arid environments in their action plans, which include the promotion of better management of water resources and protection of the integrity of waterways. Strategy work in Tunisia also identifies the need to strengthen institutional capacity to monitor and coordinate the management of water resources.

The prospect of extreme water shortages in a number of countries raises basic questions about industrial and agricultural structure and policy, including pricing policy. Integrated water resource and coastal zone management are key concerns in the environmental strategies of several countries, including Ghana, Mauritius, and several Caribbean nations. Even in countries that are relatively well endowed with water, such as India and Indonesia, issues relating to water resource management have figured prominently in environmental reports and investments.

In Indonesia threats to both water quantity and quality are addressed in a report to be published in fiscal 1991. On the island of Java shallow catchments combined with deforestation have increased the variability in runoff and caused water shortages downstream, particularly in dry years. Increasing population densities along Java's north coast are straining the capacity of coastal ecosystems to deal with municipal waste and industrial pollution, and shortages of clean water threaten both human health and industrial development. Because of high levels of municipal and industrial waste, eight major rivers on Java's north coast are regarded as significantly or seriously polluted. The massive withdrawal of groundwater in large urban centers has caused saline intrusion into shallow aquifers—a particularly serious problem since shallow wells provide most of the water for domestic use.

Allocating surface and ground water for agriculture and for municipal and industrial use is becoming an increasingly important issue in Indonesia. Future water requirements suggest possible shortages of 10 billion cubic meters in a dry year by 2010. Urban and industrial water use are expected to grow at high rates, reflecting rapid urban and industrial growth and current low levels of piped municipal water supply. Yet two thirds of the forecasted shortage could be eliminated by increasing efficiency and cost recovery. For example, unaccounted-for-water—water lost from piped systems or used without payment—represents nearly 40 percent of municipal water.

More efficient water use requires more attention to pricing policies. Charges for irrigation water in areas with water shortages and increased tariffs on groundwater in urban areas are needed to encourage conservation and help prevent overextraction. Fines and charges levied against polluters also have the potential to reduce water pollution and pay for mitigative measures. Coordination between agencies involved in water resource management should also be enhanced, and existing institutional arrangements for pollution monitoring and control should be strengthened. Water resources planning, management, and operations at the river basin and regional levels also need to take multisectoral requirements and environmental concerns into account.

- Urban, Industrial, and Agricultural Pollution. Industrial effluents, which sometimes include hazardous wastes, are becoming an increasing threat to public health and natural systems in developing countries. Water resources are especially threatened. These pollutants can usually be traced to specific point sources, but air pollution from automobiles in congested urban areas, a major nonpoint source, creates another wide range of harmful effects. The disposal of solid waste is also of growing concern, with its threats to public health, soils, waterways, and air quality. Agricultural pollution from pesticides, herbicides, and fertilizers affects soils, water systems, and the health of workers. In the absence of effective safeguards, it may also have a direct toxic effect on food supplies.

Most of the environmental action plans and strategies developed or implemented in fiscal 1990 identified urban, industrial, and agricultural pollution as significant issues. Urban pollution concerns, such as the lack of basic sanitation and the growing pressure on infrastructure from increasing urbanization and population growth, were highlighted by Algeria,

Burkina Faso, India, Rwanda, and Turkey. The effect of industrial pollution on air and water quality and solid and hazardous waste management were also identified as serious concerns in the studies in India, Mauritius, and Poland. Yugoslavia's federal environmental strategy paper, prepared with the assistance of the Bank, also emphasizes these problems. It includes a broad range of policy, legal, and institutional issues, a crucial one being the appropriate division of responsibility among various layers of government. The high levels and improper use of pesticides is a focus of the action plan in Mauritius and is of concern in other countries as well.

Jordan's energy sector study exemplifies the way in which environmental issues in this sector are approached by the Bank. Its proposed strategies for developing the energy sector include a package of incentives to promote energy conservation by providing tax incentives, improving industrial legislation, and coordinating conservation measures in the industrial, transport, and household sectors, with emphasis on efficient pricing policy. The development of renewable energy sources and improved environmental policies relating to oil shale exploitation are indicated as priorities.

The study on coal development and utilization in Thailand recommends minimizing the environmental consequences of coal production by issuing and enforcing land reclamation guidelines as well as by requiring all mine operators to submit well-defined reclamation plans, schedules, and procedures. The study also recommends that all mine operators be required to monitor dust levels and that private operators be required to implement effective waste management strategies for coal washing. A series of general recommendations are proposed for strengthening the monitoring and enforcement capacity of the National Environment Board.

On a regional level the current work on the Metropolitan Environmental Improvement Program (MEIP) recognizes the commonality of many of the urban environmental problems in the Asia Region. Formerly known as the Capital Cities Clean-up Project, the MEIP, which is supported by the United Nations Development Programme (UNDP) and the Japanese Environment Fund, aims to arrest and begin reversing environmental degradation in major Asian cities. Under the program environmental strategies are to be developed in Beijing, Colombo, Jakarta, and Manila, and a tentative agreement has been made to work in Bombay. The MEIP will include urban environmental strategy and planning, relations among private and public institutions and NGOs for environmental management, methods to monitor and manage pollution control efforts, and technologies and incentives for abating industrial pollution.

Similarly, a regional study of wastewater reuse in the Mediterranean and Middle East was substantially completed during the year. This subject is of massive economic importance in the countries concerned. The study, conducted in collaboration with the Food and Agriculture Organization (FAO) and the World Health Organization (WHO), demonstrates the crucial need for recycling and recommends detailed country strategies and the opportunities for international assistance.

A regional study of the Caribbean stresses that these countries will have to implement difficult measures during the 1990s to deal with significant development problems, including environmental sustainability issues. The critical environmental problems include marine and beach pollution, beach mining, inadequate sewerage disposal facilities, and disposal of industrial wastes. Environmental problems could become a deterrent to expanding tourism in the region and thus should be considered in formulating sectoral development policies.

Regional programs are most appropriate where several nations depend on a common resource. Ecosystems do not respect national boundaries, and the resulting physical and environmental interdependence necessitates a cross-country approach. By far the most intensive regional activity of this type conducted by the Bank is in the Mediterranean. An important inter-agency initiative is working to understand the nature, extent, and causes of environmental degradation in countries bordering the Mediterranean and to define appropriate measures and priority areas for a program of assistance. This initiative builds on extensive work done by the United Nations Environment Programme (UNEP) and is known as the Environmental Program for the Mediterranean (EPM) (Box 2-3).

• Degradation of the "Global Commons." Many environmental problems not only disregard national boundaries, but also become concerns at the global level. Such problems include loss of biodiversity; discharge of chlorofluorocarbons (CFCs) and resultant ozone depletion; other forms of atmospheric modification that create a potential for global warming; and transboundary pollution and hazardous waste disposal, particularly in the marine environment.

Resolution of many of the environmental problems highlighted in specific country environmental strategies would also contribute toward resolving these global problems and thus would confer benefits to the global community as well. Efforts must be made to identify and implement measures in which the global and national interests coincide—and there are many of them. For example, there is considerable scope for measures to increase energy efficiency, which would benefit individual countries as well as the global community. In some important cases, however, this is not so; global interests in substituting for CFCs, reducing the rate of tropical defor-

Box 2–3. The Environmental Program for the Mediterranean
(EPM)

An important report, *The Environmental Program for the Mediterranean: Preserving a Shared Heritage and Managing a Common Resource*, was published jointly by the World Bank and the European Investment Bank (EIB) in April 1990. It acknowledges the serious environmental degradation in many parts of the Mediterranean region and identifies four subjects of special concern: degradation of coastal areas, water resource management, marine pollution from oil and chemicals, and the processing, recycling, and disposal of solid and hazardous waste. Unless greater efforts to safeguard the environment are made by the Mediterranean basin states and backed by the international aid community, growing pressure on the dwindling supply of natural resources will continue the degradation in these and other areas. This in turn will damage both the quality of life and the ability of some countries to maintain adequate economic growth rates.

Concrete action supported by the EPM includes a long-term Mediterranean Environmental Technical Assistance Program, which is initially funded by the two banks, the UNDP, and the Commission of the European Communities and which will provide technical assistance for preparing projects and policy studies and the improvement of the environmental legislative and regulatory framework as well as for strengthening environmental institutions; intensified efforts by the World Bank and the EIB to identify and finance environmental projects; and initiatives to mobilize resources from other donors to protect the environment in the Mediterranean basin.

The Mediterranean countries need to develop environmental programs that focus more on resource conservation and stress preventive action rather than curative measures. Steps have already been taken by the countries of the region to address some of their environmental problems. The southern and eastern Mediterranean countries in particular must adopt urgent measures to combat pollution and manage their natural resources more efficiently to maintain the foundation for sustained economic growth.

estation, curtailing emissions of carbon dioxide, or preserving a threatened species may sometimes require actions that might not be economically justifiable for a single country. Special funding arrangements may therefore be required in such cases (see chapter 6).

Lessons from General Strategy Work

The Bank's environmental strategy work during the past year continues to reinforce the view that environmental degradation is an increasing threat to economic development, even in the short run. It is difficult, however, to assess precisely the extent to which this is so and to derive priorities among different environmental interventions. The inadequacies of traditional cost-benefit analysis and the need to supplement economic evaluation methods with qualitative judgments are in most cases quite apparent.

The studies also stress the importance of policies designed to foster a pattern of growth in developing countries that is less resource-intensive than that which has characterized development in the industrial countries. Fortunately, many opportunities exist for policies and investments in which economic and environmental objectives coincide, such as the pricing of energy at its true economic cost. Indeed many of the environmental strategy exercises conclude that inefficient economic policies are major underlying causes of environmental damage and wasted resources.

The studies highlight both the importance and the difficulty of establishing cause and effect relationships. Whereas poverty, population growth, legal and institutional factors, and economic policies might be expected to influence the ways in which resources are used—and therefore the way the environment is managed—the precise character of these relationships is rarely understood. The task of unraveling them is complex, time-consuming, and labor intensive. It is difficult, for example, to generalize about the effect of specific land tenure policies or agricultural subsidies on the environment. Similarly, while liberalized trade and a free market system will often contribute to realizing both efficiency and environmental goals, this is not always the case. Free markets are not a panacea for environmental ills, and market failure will often have to be remedied by government intervention.

The increasing threat to economic development posed by environmental degradation justifies the greater effort that will be needed if priorities are to be established systematically and if the chain of causality—and therefore the identification of appropriate policy responses—is to be handled effectively in Bank operations. In view of the range of physical, cultural, and economic variables involved, research to support policy and project recommendations will have to be very applied in nature to form a suitable foundation for the primarily operational, case-by-case focus of such work. Environmental strategy work of the kind described above formed a solid base for environmental lending in Brazil, Côte d'Ivoire, Madagascar, and Poland in fiscal 1990 and will also influence an increasing number of environmental loans in years to come.

This concern with building a solid basis for further operational activities is reflected in the outcome of the meetings for the ninth replenishment of the International Development Association (IDA-9), where donors urged that environmental action plans be completed for all IDA recipients by the end

---

Box 2–4. The Tropical Forestry Action Plan (TFAP)

An important event during the past year was a high-level review, commissioned by the FAO, of the Tropical Forestry Action Plan (TFAP). The TFAP was launched in 1985 with the support of the Bank, UNDP, FAO, and the World Resources Institute (WRI). It was designed to mobilize the resources needed for programs to manage land use, ensure the sustainability of forest-based industries, improve the supply-demand balances of fuelwood, conserve forest ecosystems, and strengthen institutions in the forestry sector.

During the fiscal year the Bank participated in a number of operations under the TFAP. A Bank team carried out a TFAP mission in Papua New Guinea that emphasized the conservation of tropical forests and recommended protecting more than 20 critical areas of biodiversity as World Heritage sites. The Bank is also participating in ongoing TFAP missions in such countries as Ethiopia, Indonesia, and Zaire.

Many criticisms have been leveled at the TFAP, including charges that it has encouraged, rather than discouraged, the destruction of tropical rainforests and that the commitment of international agencies (including the Bank) to it has been inadequate. The high-level review team, which reported its findings in June 1990, was unable to determine either how the program had influenced the rate of deforestation or whether it had affected the amount of donor support for forestry. It found that some form of TFAP was needed, but that considerable changes were necessary. Forestry development should take account of the links with the other sectors of the economy, and countries need significant help to increase their capacity to manage their forests. The TFAP should become a more successful partnership of interests and recognize global concerns, instead of being, as in the past, primarily a donor-driven device for distributing aid. The recommendations that the TFAP should give greater attention to policy reform and to local capacity building are very much in line with the Bank's policy of trying to integrate environmental concerns in general into the mainstream of its development work.

---

of the IDA-9 period. The essential principles contained in the four steps outlined at the beginning of this chapter seem appropriate to the most pressing environmental problems in the country concerned. Recent experience suggests that environmental action plans can be conducted as distinct activities with broad local and international participation and that country-based, in-depth analysis of environmental problems and their underlying causes is often a prerequisite for environmentally sound lending. It can also strengthen policy reforms and aid coordination. Significant progress in implementing environmental measures will also be achieved through addressing specific environmental problems in routine operational activities, such as economic and sector work and lending operations.

This is clearly consistent with the objective of integrating environmental concerns into Bank operations and is exemplified by several of the activities referred to previously, such as the study on environment and natural resource management in the Philippines (see Box 2-2), and the conclusions of the high-level review of the Tropical Forestry Action Plan (TFAP) (Box 2-4).

3. Policy and Research

Policy and research work on the interface between environment and development is not the sole responsibility of the Environment Department and, in keeping with the spirit of integration, now receives increasing attention throughout the Bank. Policy and research activities have been carried out primarily in the Policy, Research, and External Affairs Senior Vice Presidency (PRE), but also by staff in Operations and Finance. Within PRE, sector-specific environmental work is addressed by the appropriate sector department, while policy and research in the Environment Department and in the Development Economics Vice Presidency tends to cut across sectors. The outputs and activities described below are grouped into the priority environmental problems identified in chapter 1.

Destruction of Natural Habitats

Policy and research in this area aim to improve understanding of the economic, technical, and behavioral causes of damage to natural habitats and to use this information to implement more effective resource management policies. Improved Bank performance will require a more systematic use of existing knowledge and guidelines, better information on existing resources, and a greater understanding of the economic, social, and scientific value of threatened species. Some of the issues that have been addressed include threats to biodiversity and indigenous peoples and the effects of human settlements on natural habitats. Other areas, such as deforestation and dam construction, will often involve several of the other priority environmental problems.

In the area of biodiversity the Bank has continued to collaborate with leading environmental NGOs in a variety of initiatives, such as developing the Global Strategy for the Conservation of Biodiversity launched in late 1989 and planning the Fourth World Protected Areas Congress. A new book, *Conserving the World's Biological Diversity*, copublished by the World Bank, the International Union for Conservation of Nature and Natural

Resources (IUCN), World Resources Institute (WRI), Conservation International, and the World Wildlife Fund-US (WWF), was the subject of a recent seminar (Box 3-1).

Protected areas are coming under increasing pressure from illegal activities such as hunting, logging, burning, and agricultural encroachment. A study, "People and Parks: Linking Protected Area Management with Local Communities," was carried out jointly by the Bank, the WWF, and USAID to evaluate 18 projects in Africa, Asia, and Latin America that have taken a new approach to managing tropical parks and reserves. The study was completed during the year, and publication is expected in early fiscal 1991. In contrast to traditional approaches, which emphasize reliance on patrolling by armed guards and the forced exclusion of local people, the new projects have sought to reduce pressure on protected areas by providing alternative sources of income to local populations. Although these new approaches to managing protected areas are necessary, progress in the case-study projects has been inadequate. In general, evidence does not seem to support a reduced emphasis on park enforcement. The study recommends that renewed attention be given to strengthening the institutions responsible for managing protected areas; that substantially more serious commitments be made by governments, lenders, and donors; and that government agencies and NGOs increase their collaborative efforts to resolve the conflicts of interest between the nearby community and the park managers.

Encouraging the involvement of local people in development initiatives is also the theme of the study, "Living with Wildlife: Wildlife Utilization

---

Box 3–1. Conserving the World's Biological Diversity

Biological diversity—the total number of plant and animal genes, species, and ecosystems on earth—may have been greatest at the beginning of the industrial age. But the future looks very bleak. The explosion in the growth of the human population places ever greater demands on the planet's resources, and species are becoming extinct at the highest rate known in geological history.

Conserving the World's Biological Diversity is intended to be a primer on this subject. It supports those working directly on environmental conservation and also demonstrates to decisionmakers in other sectors that conserving biodiversity is not only their responsibility, but is also in their interest. The book explains what biological diversity is and how it can contribute to development and be integrated into policies for resource use. It then calls for concerted action among businesses, institutions, and individuals that benefit from—but are not yet shouldering responsibility for—the preservation of biological resources.

with Local Participation in Africa." The report examines the experience, potential, and constraints for developing wildlife management programs that directly involve local rural communities and bring benefits to them. It also explores the potential for using wildlife management to increase the independence and institutional capabilities of such communities and to provide greater diversity in the local economy.

A significant threat to natural habitats in some areas has been the construction of large dams without adequate attention to upstream or downstream effects. While growing populations and economic growth have increased the demands for hydropower, irrigation, and flood control, greater population densities and large existing investments make the siting of new dams more difficult. Two reviews of the Bank's performance in this area, *Dams and the Environment* and *Dam Safety and the Environment* were published during the year. The first examines the environmental factors associated with large storage dam projects and concludes that although there may well be some dams that cannot be economically justified once all costs—including environmental and social ones—are considered, analysis early in the planning process often permits protective measures to be taken that result in net economic benefits. The second report consolidates the experience of Bank staff, the consulting industry, and government agencies in the design and management of dam projects, with special emphasis on safety improvement and environmental impacts, particularly those related to water quality and public health. Both publications stress the need for improved methods of valuing environmental and social costs of dam projects in monetary terms.

Dam construction also typically involves the involuntary resettlement of local populations. The new directive on involuntary resettlement and the appointment of resettlement specialists in three of the Bank's four regional environment divisions points to the increased attention now paid to this issue (Box 3-2). The Latin America and the Caribbean Region, for example, has reviewed all projects with resettlement components and has recommended ways to improve the process. The Asia Region now has two full-time resettlement specialists, as well as a staff member attached to the resident mission in India assigned to resettlement matters. In the Africa Region attention has focused on resettlement issues associated with forestry development projects.

In addition to the activities that have been completed, several initiatives are in progress and are expected to contribute to the future development of the Bank's strategy for protecting natural habitats. Indigenous ecological knowledge and land use practices are some of the issues addressed in the on-going revision of the Bank's guideline on "Tribal Peoples in Bank-Financed Projects." A group of Bank sociologists and anthropologists has

---

Box 3–2. Operational Directive on Involuntary Resettlement

A new operational directive on involuntary resettlement, released in June 1990, broadens the treatment of resettlement issues beyond hydropower and irrigation projects to all types of investments. The revised directive was based on more than a decade of Bank experience and sociological evaluation of resettlement. It emphasizes the need to minimize involuntary resettlement; to provide people displaced by a project with means to improve—or at least restore—their former living standards, earning capacity, and production levels; to involve both resettlers and hosts in resettlement activities; to provide a time-bound resettlement plan; and to develop valuation and compensation principles for land and other assets affected by the project. It also takes note of some of the unintended effects of involuntary resettlement on the environment, such as deforestation and watershed deterioration, and suggests ways to avoid such consequences.

---

begun to revise the guideline, incorporating the experience gained since the original one was drafted in 1982. The objective of the revision is to encourage the design of projects to take into account the specific socioeconomic, cultural, and environmental conditions of the world's tribal or indigenous peoples and incorporate them more effectively into programs to conserve and develop fragile or threatened habitats. In revising the guideline, the group will draw on the expertise and experience of the Bank's four regions and the work being done in this area by other UN agencies, such as the International Labour Organisation, which revised the International Convention on Indigenous and Tribal Populations in 1989.

Finally, a major initiative begun during the year was preparation of a new forestry policy paper. The paper will provide Bank staff and country personnel with guidelines for effective forest management, especially as it relates to curbing deforestation and the loss of natural habitat. The policy paper will emphasize sustainable utilization of all forest resources, including moist and dry tropical forests as well as temperate forests, and will address the extremely complex issue of the tradeoffs between economic and environmental objectives. Environmental issues to be examined are biodiversity and the conservation of tropical forests, global warming implications, watershed protection, and the role of trees in sustainable agricultural systems.

Land Degradation

Work in this area aims to improve understanding of the extent, causes, and economic consequences of soil erosion and desertification in order to improve agricultural and land management projects and policies. Policy and applied research carried out during the year revolved primarily around farm policies and incentives, land tenure issues, and community participation.

A series of activities on drylands was carried out in fiscal 1990. The paper, "Dryland Degradation Measurement Techniques," provides practical guidelines for evaluating projects in dryland areas. It proposes alternative definitions for drylands degradation and methods for assessing their productivity and resilience. Another paper, "World Bank Drylands Management Study," reviews the lessons of experience in drylands management. It identifies the steps required to improve dryland production systems, assesses available information on dryland management, and sets out areas needing further study. It also reviews successful projects and summarizes the constraints facing designers and implementors of dryland interventions. In addition the proceedings of the Professional Workshop on Dryland Management held in May 1989 were published. The main issues covered include dryland management, water management and soil fertility, policy requirements for improved land management, the effects of off-farm earnings and migration, and community participation.

The difficulty of identifying critical variables in soil management is addressed in *Soil Conservation in Developing Countries: Project and Policy Intervention*. Factors usually associated with successful soil conservation include the existence of both on- and off-farm income; access to low-cost credit, especially when targeted to conservation; a high level of education among farmers; access to sound technical advice; and secure land tenure. The study identifies needs for empirical research to refine understanding of the most important factors in land conservation systems. Some of the general conclusions of this study—the importance of local participation, training, and the need to consider social and cultural factors—are applicable to a wide range of environmental issues. This is illustrated in a major study of social forestry (Box 3-3).

The booklet, *Vetiver Grass: The Hedge against Erosion*, was also published during the year and advocates this low-cost, simple, and tested way to conserve water and reduce soil erosion. Using a uniquely durable and adaptable grass, *Vetiveria zizanioides*, as a contour hedge, this technology is being adopted in Africa, Asia, and Latin America. It may be more successful in fighting erosion than traditional, costly systems and is likely to play a key role in rehabilitating degraded lands and reducing the loss of soil nutrients in rainfed areas. A scientific audit of its properties and of any adverse environmental impacts is being carried out for the Bank by the National Science Foundation in Washington, D.C.

**Box 3–3. People and Trees: The Role of Social Forestry
in Sustainable Development**

Trees—and not just the wood products that come from them—can help
increase the sustainability of rural development. The productive use of trees
can reduce environmental degradation, halt the decline of agricultural productivity, alleviate shortages in the supply of fuelwood, and reduce unem-
ployment. An enormous amount of investment in forestry and tree growing
will be needed in the coming years to balance the requirements for environmental stability and the local demand for forest and tree projects.

Social forestry—as distinguished from industrial and large-scale government forestry—is the involvement of local, generally rural, people in growing
trees for their own use. Information needed to improve education and training
programs for social forestry is brought together in *People and Trees: The Role of
Social Forestry in Sustainable Development*. The book relates developing
countries' recent experiences with social forestry programs and projects, and
the material is presented in a manner useful for people working in this field.
Two of the most important conditions for success are a high level of local
participation and strong political commitment to long-term solutions to current problems. The book highlights some fundamental issues in social forestry
and suggests ways to resolve them to reduce the time between the planning
and successful implementation of sustainable programs.

The economic consequences of land degradation is a key topic in the
major publication, *Sub-Saharan Africa: From Crisis to Sustainable Growth*,
which integrates environmental issues into its basic analysis of economic
and social conditions in Africa. Land degradation has a direct bearing on
agriculture, food security, and energy production in the region. Deforestation, for example, outstrips the rate of new tree planting by 28 to 1. As a
result 55 million Africans face acute scarcity of fuelwood, and much of the
continent's unique animal and plant life, as well as its preagricultural
cultures, is threatened with extinction. More than 80 percent of Africa's
rangelands and cropped areas in dryland regions may be affected by soil
degradation and consequent fertility losses. The report asserts that conservation will fail unless it appeals to farmers' self-interest. But farmers, forest
dwellers, and pastoralists will become interested in conservation only if
price, exchange rate, fiscal, and other distortions are removed and tenure
conditions and productivity are improved. Better agricultural practices,
institutions, and policies are urgently needed. The report urges that responsibility for resource management be transferred to local communities.

Also in fiscal 1990 the Operations Evaluation Department published a
review of the Bank's economic sector work and project experience in

managing renewable resources. The review, *Renewable Resource Management in Agriculture*, analyzes the results of 335 completed agriculture and forestry projects in the tropics. In addition it examines the findings in 12 country studies representing the three principal tropical ecological zones: the humid tropical lowlands, desert and semiarid lands, and mountain watersheds. The report reviews the constraints to effective resource management both within the Bank and within its member countries and the variety of options available for further action.

Work in progress tends to focus on the economic consequences of land degradation and on identifying promising legal and economic incentives to improve land management. A methodology to identify the on-site costs of soil erosion, using Mali as a case study, is being developed. In another study the results of fieldwork carried out in fiscal 1990 on the economic framework of smallholder agriculture in Kenya and, in particular, on the range of tree-growing practices, are now being analyzed. This study focuses on the evolution of land tenure systems and their effect on tree growing as well as on the pricing and policy processes that produce innovation in land use and in turn encourage (or discourage) particular tree-growing practices. Land use inventories were used to categorize the extent to which particular tree-growing strategies and other land-use strategies have been adopted or maintained. Surveys and interviews were used to collect social and economic information on factor endowments and use.

Land tenure is the subject of an ongoing study that examines the effects of tenure conditions on resource management. In many countries indigenous institutions function alongside formal ones to regulate access to and use of land and natural resources. The study hopes to clarify the role of these indigenous institutions in environmental management and to highlight both their strengths and weaknesses in the face of changing economic and social conditions. Case studies of Madagascar, Niger, and north Yemen are substantially completed, and the study should lead to policy proposals for Bank operations that touch on land tenure issues.

A large number of current and planned projects in the Asia Region deal with the associated issues of upland productivity and environment and are motivated by concern for the downstream effects of watershed degradation, such as flooding and sedimentation. The Environment and Asia Technical Departments have collaborated on a study of watershed development to be published in early fiscal 1991. The study will cover strategic issues in watershed development, techniques for soil and moisture conservation, revegetation, economic analysis of soil conservation technologies, the economic aspect of off-farm soil conservation structures, and land tenure issues. The study will also develop a framework for planning, monitoring, and evaluating watershed development projects. Counter to popular opinion, the study argues that reforestation may not be an effective strategy in heavily populated areas. Rather, soil and water conservation will have to result from improved agricultural practices.

Degradation and Depletion of Fresh Water Resources

Problems of water availability and quality are emerging as limiting constraints to development. They are of increasing concern in almost every country and are likely to become particularly severe in the decade ahead. A review of policy and research activities in the Bank, however, reveals that to date insufficient attention has been paid the problems of fresh water depletion and degradation. Research already done on this subject, both inside and outside the Bank, needs to be put to use in country economic and sector work and in projects. In many countries impending water shortages threaten economic growth and call for government review of national industrial and agricultural policies. The traditional sectoral approach needs to be replaced by an integrated approach to water resource management, involving agricultural, energy, industrial, and municipal uses. Guidelines and state-of-the-art reviews, training, and implementation of well-known techniques in operations should also receive high priority.

The Bank is now developing an interdepartmental work program aimed at achieving a more integrated approach to water management in its operations. A two-year study of comprehensive water resource management policy will examine and develop policy guidelines for some of the main issues affecting the management of, and investments in, the water sector. It will cover several intersectoral issues: water scarcity caused by either a physical lack of water or by inappropriate socioeconomic and institutional allocation methods; water pollution and environmental degradation caused by industrial and urban wastes, agrochemical residuals in surface or groundwater, aquifer salinization, and other ecological factors; and conflicts in water allocation between traditional agricultural use and growing urban and industrial needs.

In addition to proposing policy guidelines for the Bank's project work, the study will address issues relevant to the policy dialogue between the Bank and its borrowers and will analyze water resource issues for the 21st century. The study will involve several departments in PRE (including Agriculture and Rural Development, Environment, Infrastructure and Urban Development, International Economics, and the Economic Development Institute) and the regional technical and country departments. Country studies, starting with the Europe, Middle East, and North Africa Region, will provide guidance on water resource management and practices and will reflect the differing status of current regional and country policies and program objectives on water resource management.

Complementing these studies, a research proposal aims to develop a new analytical model to help identify optimal investment strategies for irrigation and agricultural development in Middle Eastern countries. Previous lending programs will be studied, and current and future projects examined, to help develop a sound long-term water policy for the Middle East and to select alternative strategies that can substantially reduce the degree to which water will be a major constraint to economic development in the region. The final phase of the research will implement and evaluate the decision-aiding model, using Jordan as a case study.

Research has also been initiated on a topic of great importance in many parts of the world, namely the problems of waterlogging and salinity that often follow, sometimes after many years, from irrigation schemes. The research will review existing knowledge on the most critical processes underlying the progressive deterioration of irrigated lands; define the vulnerable combinations of soils, water, crops, and climatic conditions; identify, where relevant, design deficiencies or flaws that contribute to this deterioration; ascertain the need for drainage and its optimal timing; and analyze the role of current and alternative policies in either preventing or ameliorating waterlogging and salinity. In the face of what appears to be the inevitable deterioration of irrigation systems resulting from waterlogging and salinity, the research hopes to identify the appropriate combination of irrigation and drainage projects, on the one hand, and water management policies, on the other. The research will also provide guidelines relating to the mix of preventive and remedial projects and policies. Egypt and Pakistan have been selected for in-depth data collection and analytical work.

Urban, Industrial, and Agricultural Pollution

Rapidly growing urban populations and increasing industrialization are leading to massive pollution problems in many countries. In rural areas pollution and health effects from the inappropriate use of pesticides are also an increasing concern. The Bank has conducted a considerable amount of policy and research work in this area over the years, as evidenced by existing guidelines and by the number of loans for pollution reduction. Research has concentrated on water, sanitation, and solid waste disposal in urban areas; industrial pollution control measures; and pesticide guidelines and standards. Priorities for the future include updating industrial guidelines for Bank staff, devoting more attention to managing air quality, identifying economic incentives for pollution control, and reviewing the lessons from the Bank's operational experience with pollution control measures.

As in water resource management, there is a growing need for an integrated approach to activities in the area of pollution control. In a review of 71 Bank-supported projects with components for municipal solid waste management, the Infrastructure and Urban Development Department concludes that the lack of a more comprehensive approach has limited the effect of many of these projects. In many instances improvements in solid waste management have been limited to equipment procurement, and only about half of the projects provided environmentally safe disposal facilities. The strengthening of local institutions responsible for solid waste management also requires more attention.

Air quality management is a subject of rapidly growing concern, not only because of the considerable local damage to public health, buildings, and crops, but also because of its regional and global impact. Diagnostic studies of air pollution in Ankara and Mexico City were initiated in the Environment Department; a review of air pollution in Beijing was completed; and other studies on health effects of air pollution and pollution control strategies were carried out. The papers conclude that since developing countries face ever-growing populations and rising expectations for better living conditions, they cannot contemplate eliminating economic activities that contribute to a polluted environment. The most promising option available is to embrace a comprehensive package of economic and educational policies that encourage energy conservation, mass transport, nonpolluting industrial processes, and balanced urban growth. Economic measures include eliminating perverse incentives for energy consumption through correct pricing of electricity and rationalizing industrial production processes. Other proposed interventions address more basic problems—such as high population growth rates and rapid rural-to-urban migration, which impose a heavy burden on an ecosystem's ability to supply resources or absorb wastes.

Transportation is a major contributor to air pollution and is the subject of a study on land transport and air pollution in developing countries prepared by the Infrastructure and Urban Development Department. "Environmental and Ecological Considerations in Land Transport" reviews the current importance of motor vehicles as a cause of the various air pollution problems, assesses the negative effects of this pollution, reviews the efforts under way to bring about improvements, and identifies future research needs. To reduce and maintain vehicle pollution at acceptable levels, a multifaceted strategy is proposed and includes improved standards for new vehicles, inspection and maintenance strategies, improved fuel quality, continuous efforts in traffic management and in land use and transportation planning, and, in the long term, fundamentally new power plant technologies and fuel substitution.

The Infrastructure and Urban Development Department also published a technical paper, "The Environmentally Sound Disposal of Dredged Materials," which specifically addresses the various disposal options available today as well as future directions. The paper discusses the scope of the problem, intergovernmental agreements regulating pollution, disposal options, possible future action, and the tradeoffs between cost, practicality, and reduction of environmental impact.

Issues in agricultural pollution have also been the subject of several research and policy activities (Box 3-4). In 1985 the Bank became the first donor agency to adopt specific guidelines on the selection and use of pesticides in its lending program. After several years of operational experience with the guidelines, it became apparent that an update was warranted, and a panel of external advisers, including representatives from the environmental community and the pesticide industry, drafted a new set of guidelines and advised the Bank on issues relating to pest management and pesticide use. The revision will make the Bank's policies easier for Bank staff and borrowers to implement and will expand guidelines in particular areas, such as sectoral lending, that have become increasingly important in the Bank's operations. The new directive, entitled "Agricultural Pest Management," will include as a subannex the updated "Guidelines on Selection and Use of Pesticides." A third element, "Guidelines on Procurement of Pesticides," has also been prepared and will be incorporated into the Bank's general procurement guidelines. The operational directive is expected to be formally adopted during fiscal 1991.

Box 3–4. Integrated Pest Management in African Agriculture

An important technical paper, "Integrated Pest Management in African Agriculture," uses a series of case studies on subsistence-level production, high-input monoculture, and systems in the process of intensification to show that this technology is feasible for all types of African farming systems. The importance of a strong extension system to provide a link between farmers and researchers is emphasized, as is the role of donors in building local research and extension capabilities, educating extension workers and farmers about the benefits of the approach, training them in specific methodologies, and ensuring that the necessary products, equipment, and infrastructure are present. Donors can also encourage and help governments to establish a policy environment that gives farmers the incentive and capability to implement a sustainable approach to pest management.

Because the Bank has a comparative advantage in economic analysis, future work in the field of pollution control will continue to emphasize such topics as cost-benefit studies and the use of economic incentives. Considerable attention will also be devoted to management, institutional, and regulatory issues. In fact these will be the central themes of a strategy paper on urban management and environment to be prepared by the Infrastructure and Urban Development Department with assistance from the UNDP. Aided by in-depth case studies, the project will assess environment problems that affect human health, such as water and air pollution, and problems that pose a more long-term threat to resources and development, such as groundwater depletion, land degradation, and improper disposal of hazardous waste. The project will recommend criteria for adopting priority curative actions to reduce public health risks. Preventive measures—for example, pricing resources to discourage their excessive use and improvements in regulations for environmental protection and enforcement procedures—will also be suggested. Research on the effects of urban environmental conditions on health and on the role of the private sector in solid waste management services has already begun.

Degradation of the "Global Commons"

The prospect of global warming, threats to the ozone layer, decreasing biodiversity, hazardous wastes, and pollution of international waters all give additional justification for most of the tasks already referred to. A major challenge, however, is to keep staff up to date with continually evolving scientific information on the extent of these problems so that the Bank can develop appropriate sectoral and macroeconomic responses and can continue to play a major role in international initiatives, such as the proposed Global Environmental Facility. The integration of sound scientific information with policy issues has been one of the important objectives of work in this area.

Various aspects of the "global commons" problem were addressed in policy and research during the year. A collaborative effort involving several departments and led by the Bank's principal science and technology advisor, resulted in the publication of *The Greenhouse Effect: Implications for Economic Development* (Box 3-5).

To get a better understanding of the implications of international proposals on the greenhouse issue for developing countries, a major study is under way in the International Economics Department. It will provide background information for a more informed discussion of issues such as

---

Box 3–5. The Greenhouse Effect: Implications for Economic Development

This study presents a scientific perspective on the issue of global climatic change and establishes a comprehensive framework for a response to the implications for natural resource conservation and economic development. An overview and critique of the sometimes conflicting scientific literature and opinion on the greenhouse effect are presented with the related theoretical and empirical evidence and prospects for global climatic change. A set of conclusions address policy and research issues for the Bank as well as for the development community as a whole. The greatest opportunities to mitigate the threat of global warming are seen to lie in the energy sector, where the opportunities for public and private gains in energy efficiency are compelling and where significant improvements can be made with very little incremental costs to the countries concerned. In other words, economically efficient measures are often environmentally positive.

---

emission limits and compensatory funding, especially as they pertain to developing countries. The study will also examine the implications on commodity markets of policies proposed by the international community to reduce greenhouse gases.

Cross-Cutting Issues

The need to integrate environmental concerns into the mainstream of country economic and sector work continues to be of overwhelming importance and has generated a variety of general cross-cutting issues for research and policy work. A recent book, *Environmental Management and Economic Development*, written by Bank staff and consultants, surveys the key economic issues in managing natural resources in developing countries (Box 3-6). One of the topics addressed is the case for more systematic incorporation of the environment into national income accounts. Ongoing work in the Bank on this issue builds on the conceptual approaches published last year in *Environmental Accounting for Sustainable Development*. Ways to adjust conventional national income accounting procedures to more accurately reflect environmental considerations, in particular the costs of resource depletion and of defensive environmental expenditures, were investigated. A review of the environmental and natural resource accounting experience of industrial countries has been completed, and an environmental and natural resource accounting study for Mexico has begun.

Box 3–6. Environmental Management and Economic Development

Environmental degradation threatens the productivity of the agricultural and forest resources on which developing countries depend for their economic growth. The problem is most pervasive in the poorest countries, where poverty and population pressures compel people to deplete the natural resources to meet their immediate needs for survival. Forests are burned to make room for food crops, and the soil is depleted when cow dung must be used for cooking fuel instead of fertilizer—thus both the environment and prospects for economic betterment suffer.

Much environmental damage, however, is the result of shortsighted policies and lack of information—as when insecure land tenure, artificially low prices for farm commodities, and illiteracy keep farmers from practicing soil conservation. This relation between the environment and economic development is analyzed in *Environmental Management and Economic Development*. The book illustrates in detail many typical problems and points to the options available to developing countries to protect—and even enhance—their natural environment while continuing to improve economic and social welfare. Contrary to other recent studies, the authors find cause for some optimism: governments are turning their attention to these issues, examining the environmental effects of various economic policies, and taking steps to preserve their natural resources and prevent further damage. The fundamental argument is that systematic evaluations and assessments of economic costs and benefits often show that sensible policies and actions that protect the environment can at the same time contribute to economic progress.

Experience gained from Bank operations, in particular from environmental strategy work, highlights the importance of price signals in determining the way in which environmental resources are used. The environmental problems of the Eastern European countries perhaps provide the most dramatic evidence of this. Countries of the Organisation for Economic Co-operation and Development (OECD) have also recognized the importance of prices, as exemplified by policy developments—such as the application of pollution charges—in recent years. A recent OECD report notes that countries are placing increasing reliance on economic instruments and environmental taxes, building on the "polluter pays principle." Unless prices of raw materials and products properly reflect social costs (long-run marginal social costs) and unless prices can be assigned to the air, water, and land resources that currently serve as cost-free receptacles for the waste products of society, resources will be used inefficiently and environmental pollution will increase. The OECD is currently preparing guidelines for developing and applying pollution charges, taxes, and other economic instruments directed at air, water, and soil pollutants, as well as noise and solid waste problems. It is also developing principles to facilitate the introduction, use, and modification of economic instruments.

Experience from OECD countries is important, but monitoring, enforcement, and regulatory capacity tend to be much weaker in developing countries than in industrial ones. This suggests that environmental policy instruments appropriate for developing countries may differ systematically from those used in industrial ones. Other things being equal, developing countries should probably rely less on "command and control" techniques or on the enforcement of environmental conditions associated with projects. Similarly, the use of environmental charges or fees, which themselves require an elaborate monitoring and enforcement capability, will often be less feasible in developing countries. Because the institutional and regulatory costs of dealing with environmentally unsound projects or activities on a case-by-case basis are so high, efforts must be made to identify underlying causes of those problems and to introduce remedial measures accordingly. This may involve interventions related to energy, materials, or agricultural policy.

In light of this, preparation has begun for a research project to be conducted jointly between the Environment and the Country Economics Departments on the role of fiscal incentives in achieving environmental objectives. This work will be an important element of Bank efforts to integrate environmental concerns into macroeconomic work and will be carried out in close collaboration with the Environment Division in the Europe, Middle East, and North Africa Region. Largely through case studies on Hungary, Tunisia, Turkey, and Yugoslavia, the project will identify the appropriate mix of direct incentive systems (such as effluent charges or stumpage fees) and indirect fiscal interventions (such as taxation or subsidization of agricultural or industrial inputs or outputs). The potential for "green taxes," perhaps to substitute for taxes on income and capital, will be assessed.

Another important research project addresses the links between economic policies and the environment. This study on economic growth and trade policy in western Africa and the implications of the degradation of the vegetation cover is being carried out in the Country Economics Department and assesses the extent to which the observed fall in agricultural productivity in Côte d'Ivoire and Ghana during the past decade is related to the serious degradation of natural vegetation that has occurred. More specifically, the study is concerned with the likely effects on the environment of trade policies implemented during the 1980s. This research should help the Bank to understand some of the potential environmental consequences of its trade policy recommendations and their effects on economic growth through environmental mechanisms. The project is now in its second phase; the first phase has been completed and presents a theoretical model and analysis of village and household data. Satellite remote sensing data and data on agricultural production in the chosen areas have been collected and are being processed. Preliminary results are expected in early fiscal 1991.

This project is restricted to analyzing the trade policies of developing countries. The impact of the trade policies of industrial countries on economic growth in the developing world—and the associated environmental effects—is a topic that warrants further investigation.

A study tracing the evolution of environmental economics in recent years and its relevance for developing countries is also being prepared and will be completed in fiscal 1991. Work has also continued on integrating economic and geographically based data to investigate the links between economic and other policies and environmental change, particularly for forest and land resources.

The feasibility of sustainable economic development is a central issue. A major conference, Ecological Economics of Sustainability: Making Local and Short-Term Goals Consistent with Global and Long-Term Goals, was sponsored jointly by the Environment Department and the USAID. Topics included the ecological economics of sustainable development and sustainable agriculture, managing the commons for sustainability, modeling ecological economic systems, energy analysis and ecological economics, policy implications of ecological economic analysis, measurement and valuation of natural resources, ecological economic solutions to environmental degradation, and incentives and disincentives for achieving sustainability.

Basic assumptions underlying the feasibility of sustainable development are considered in an Environment Department Working Paper entitled "Allocation, Distribution, and Scale as Determinants of Environmental Degradation." The paper analyzes environmental degradation in three small Latin American countries—Costa Rica, El Salvador, and Haiti—in terms of a basic issue that confronts the global community, namely the feasibility of continued economic development given the rapid rates of population growth that are observed in the developing world. The general conclusion is that excessive scale (population multiplied by per capita resource use) and maldistribution (concentrated land ownership) are more basic causes of environmental degradation in all three countries than is misallocation (distorted prices), although the latter remains a very important indirect cause. The policy implication is that more emphasis should be given to scale reduction (especially population control) and redistribution (especially land reform). These are not novel policy recommendations, but they are different from the policies actually followed in the countries studied.

The links between environmental degradation and poverty are as yet poorly understood. The increasing concentration of the poor in fragile and often marginal areas is underscored in the 1990 *World Development Report* on poverty. Rather than provide evidence for a causal relationship between poverty and environmental degradation, the report emphasizes the many indirect links between poverty and the environment. These include population pressure, diminished access to land and other natural resources, and a series of ill-advised government policies. Among the strategies proposed to break the vicious cycle of poverty and environmental degradation are increased investments in education and extension, in basic needs such as health care, and in sanitation and safe drinking water. Government policies on access to land have also been a central ingredient in the equation linking poverty and the environment. Success stories in poverty reduction and environmental protection do exist, however, and some are reviewed in the report.

Certain sectoral concerns may also fall under the category of cross-cutting issues. For example, public health may be profoundly affected by the environmental consequences of activities in other sectors and by macroeconomic policies. A review of the effects of development projects and policies on health has been conducted jointly by the Bank and WHO. The study, which was completed during the year and will be the subject of a joint WHO-World Bank publication entitled *Health Impacts of Development Policies*, assesses the literature and operational evidence on the effect of macroeconomic and sectoral policies and projects on health. Several country studies conducted by WHO with Bank assistance will follow.

In the energy sector, conservation and efficiency concerns also frequently cut across sectoral lines, as illustrated by much of the work of the Energy Sector Management Assistance Program (ESMAP). In fiscal 1990 ESMAP produced a series of papers for the fourth annual meeting of ESMAP donors, which addressed several topics: greenhouse gases and global warming, energy efficiency strategies for developing countries, household and rural energy and the environment, and natural gas and the environment. After the meeting ESMAP also announced a major initiative on energy and environmental research that will focus primarily on energy efficiency and alternative fuels.

"A Review of the Treatment of Environmental Aspects of Bank Energy Projects" covers 1978 to 1989 and also highlights cross-cutting concerns such as resettlement and pollution control. The review, conducted by the Industry and Energy Department during the fiscal year, states that there has been considerable improvement in addressing resettlement and pollution issues in recent years, as evidenced by a growing number of projects with environmental protection components or explicit objectives. A new problem, however, has emerged—namely the growing gap in environmental standards between projects financed by the Bank and investments financed from other sources. The study points to the increased cost of project development and monitoring when resettlement and environmental issues are seriously addressed in energy lending.

Risk management continued to be an important part of the Environment Department work program and included research on the costs and benefits of natural disaster recovery, reviews of Bank experience in funding emergency recovery, and utilization of traditional community responses for flood mitigation. During the year a colloquium was held at the Bank on the environment and disaster management. About 150 international experts participated in the meeting, which brought to the fore the links between environmental degradation, poverty, and disasters. The main goals of the colloquium were to discuss the lessons learned in environmental management concerning disaster prevention and mitigation—particularly in view of issues such as global climatic change—and to identify the most appropriate strategies to reduce the vulnerability of sectors such as agriculture, energy, and infrastructure.

Also during the year, the paper "Analyzing the Costs and Benefits of Natural Disaster Responses in the Context of Development" was issued. It focuses on the disproportionately high impact of disasters on developing countries, in which losses to gross national product are about 20 times greater than in industrial countries. The cost-effectiveness of disaster prevention versus disaster recovery is also analyzed. A set of guidelines to staff on emergency recovery assistance was issued in November 1989 following a collaborative effort between the Environment and the Central Operations Departments.

A review of Bank activities in emergency lending is being prepared to provide a framework for future work in this area. It will analyze past experience in disaster-related activities, identify the lessons learned, and recommend measures for disaster prevention, mitigation, and recovery in Bank lending. The review is expected be become a major tool in supporting operational activities, such as the current activities in China, India, and Western Samoa and those under preparation in Iran.

Other activities in progress include work on an "Environmental Manual for Power Development" to provide a common and mutually agreed approach for systematically appraising the environmental consequences of power development. Building on a state-of-the-art review completed during the year, the manual will provide decisionmakers with data to help them analyze the environmental consequences of power system components. The identification of environmentally sensitive issues, their costs and tradeoffs, and the scope for mitigatory measures will all be addressed.

A bias against environmental projects or conservation measures has been encouraged in the past by the difficulties of valuing environmental goods and services and predicting future conditions. At the same time the increasing and genuine concern about environmental degradation may well result in overinvestment in activities claiming to be environmentally benign; yet, as in the past, prediction and evaluation problems make objective tests of such claims difficult. Although monetary values cannot be relied on entirely as decision criteria, valuation processes should involve systematic and rigorous analysis of environmental costs and benefits that have often been ignored in the past, and nonmonetary values must also be included in project justification and macroeconomic policy. An exercise is currently under way in the Environment Department that involves a review of state-of-the-art developments in analyzing the costs and benefits of the environmental consequences of projects and policies, extended to incorporate nonmonetary variables into such calculations.

Institutional problems in their many forms—including inefficient public agencies, inadequate legislation, and cultural factors—have been identified in various environmental issues papers and action plans. A major research program on this subject, initiated by the Environment and Legal Departments, aims to better understand how local institutional structures (including laws, policies, and organizations) help or hinder attempts to formulate and implement policies and programs to improve environmental quality or to manage natural resources. The project will draw lessons from a series of country studies about the strengths and weaknesses of various traditional institutional arrangements (such as ministries and other regulatory approaches) and the relationships between these and other policy interventions that may reinforce environmental management. Local experts have completed preliminary fieldwork for a case study of Costa Rica, which will support country operations. This first test case, combined with selected work already under way in other country departments, will provide the basis for a working paper outlining a methodology for assessing institutional capacity in environmental matters and options for better integrating environmental issues into development policies.

The comparative advantage of the Bank is clearly with economic, institutional, and behavioral research as applied to environmental problems, and the range of unknowns—that is, researchable activities—is massive. Up to now the Bank has proceeded cautiously in this area because of the need to define research priorities carefully and because of the view that the areas in which knowledge needs to be improved tend to be more empirical than conceptual. In this context, application of generally accepted economic principles to the operational needs of countries should take priority over pure research. As outlined above, the Bank's growing environmental research program continues to stress applied work. The intellectual effort devoted, for example, to the innovative application of standard economic analysis to environmental questions in operational work, will continue to command priority in the foreseeable future. In more technical areas, in which the Bank clearly does not have a comparative advantage in conducting research, there is a growing need to keep staff up to date with rapidly evolving developments through state-of-the-art papers and guidance to staff. Associated with this is the issue of staff training, which is discussed in chapter 5.

4. Environmental Lending Operations

Environmental concerns have been addressed in many aspects of the Bank's lending operations in the past year. During the fiscal year 11 loans for free-standing environmental projects were approved, and 107 loans—about 50 percent of all projects approved—contained environmental components; 4 structural adjustment and 5 sector adjustment loans also specifically addressed environmental objectives. Lending in the energy, industry, agriculture, forestry, and population sectors has continued to place increased emphasis on the environment. Further along in the project cycle, monitoring and evaluation functions have now become more important.

Free-Standing Environmental Projects

The Bank has increased lending for projects that specifically address environmental concerns. The 1989 report to the Development Committee stated that approximately 30 projects with a major focus on environment were in the pipeline for fiscal 1990–92. In fact there will be significantly more—about 45 during the next three years. Many of them cut across sectors and emphasize institutional strengthening. Most will address some aspect of land degradation; 20 or more will concern protection of natural habitats; at least 10 will address the degradation, depletion, and management of water resources; and a dozen will focus on aspects of urban, industrial, or agricultural pollution.

Eleven free-standing environmental loans were approved during the past year. Most of these loans were to African countries and were oriented toward conservation of natural habitats and tropical forests. Such projects are inherently very complex and require major borrower and staff effort in design and implementation. Significant difficulties are faced in dealing with complex institutional arrangements, cultural and social concerns, and the perennial issue of valuation of the services provided by tropical forests; in many cases staff have had to grapple with difficulties posed by the

49

existence of significant tradeoffs between environmental and short-term economic objectives. Many of the Bank's recent projects have introduced innovative approaches to addressing tropical forestry issues and to reconciling ecological sustainability with the need for economic development and growth.

Legal and institutional deficiencies often pose serious threats to the sustainable management of forests. Forestry projects often stress the need to improve the legislative framework and fiscal incentive systems in the forestry and wildlife sectors as well as the importance of strengthening institutional capacity to implement environmental protection measures. Major components of the Natural Resource Management Project in the Central African Republic ($19 million IDA credit), for example, include implementation of a revised forestry code to define the various types of forests in the public domain; more clear definition of the customary rights to forest resources held by rural populations; and introduction of artisanal permits for the commercial exploitation of firewood from natural forests. The Forestry II Project in Indonesia ($20 million) aims to support policy and institutional reforms for improving forest management through better concession management, external inspection, and an auditing system to monitor compliance with government regulations; the project also formulates a national plan to guide land allocation and investment. The establishment of institutions and systems for managing forestry and fisheries resources is also central to the Forestry and Fisheries Management Project in Guinea ($8.0 million IDA credit), which includes a pilot operation to register land rights on the borders of the humid forest reserves.

Management plans are another central component of most forestry projects. The Forest Resource Management and Development project in Zimbabwe ($14.5 million) contains a rural forestry program that includes a pilot operation in woodland management. It also includes plans for wildlife management, forest grazing, and the development of sustainable commercial forestry operations. Similarly, to improve forest management, the Forestry II Project in Morocco ($49 million) includes support for forest inventory and demarcation as well as formulation of a forest management plan and a national reforestation plan, which will encourage the development and testing of new forestry techniques. The projects in the Central African Republic, Guinea, and Indonesia also emphasize improved forest management. In the Central African Republic, for example, the project requires forest companies to prepare a management plan for the concession for which they seek a permit, which addresses issues such the environmental impact of future logging activities and their participation in reforestation programs. In the Indonesia project, research support on the sustainable management of natural forests and the reforestation of degraded land is provided. In Guinea the forestry and fisheries project calls for integrated resource management plans for fisheries resources to address access to fishing zones, conditions for harvesting, and the limitation of catch levels.

The demarcation of forest borders is often a first step in conservation and management plans. The Guinea forestry project provides support for the demarcation, protection, and management of about 150,000 hectares of humid forests and 160,000 hectares of dry forest. The Forestry Sector Project in the Côte d'Ivoire ($80 million) is also designed to substantially check forest destruction and to protect wildlife through demarcating 1.5 million hectares of rain forests, preparing forestry management plans, and strengthening surveillance. The project supports buffer zones around forest areas and plans for agricultural development and land use in adjoining areas as well as the strengthening of surveillance infrastructure and equipment. Concerns regarding the potential opening of some 700,000 hectares of tropical forest to logging activities have been addressed, and the project will produce sustainable management plans for areas that had previously been open to uncontrolled logging.

Technical assistance and training are often required to strengthen institutional capabilities in the forestry sector; this is recognized by several of the projects mentioned above, including the projects in Guinea and the Zimbabwe. Research needs are addressed in Côte d'Ivoire's forestry project through the establishment of a research program for natural forest silviculture and management, industrial plantation techniques, and agroforestry.

Some free-standing environmental loans, such as Brazil's national environment project, cover a range of multisectoral issues (Box 4-1). In Madagascar, the Environment I Project ($26 million IDA credit) is the product of intensive and ambitious preparatory work that takes a comprehensive approach to environmental problems in the country. Implementing the first 5-year stage of the 15-year environmental action program, the project includes components for protecting and managing biodiversity, soil conservation, watershed areas, agroforestry, reforestation, institutional support, land titling, and marine and coastal ecosystems research, as well as establishing a geographic information system in priority areas. Environmental education, training, and research are also supported under the project.

Water management and pollution are two of the other prominent environmental concerns addressed by free-standing projects in Côte d'Ivoire, Madagascar, and Poland during fiscal 1990 (Box 4-2). Flood protection and the related problem of wastewater disposal are the focus of the Tana Plain Development Project in Madagascar ($30.5 million IDA credit). In the Abidjan area of the Côte d'Ivoire a major concern is the dumping of urban wastes and industrial effluents into the Ebrie lagoon. The Abidjan Lagoon

---

Box 4–1. The Environmental Project in Brazil

Institutional strengthening is a key objective of the loan for the Environmental Project in Brazil ($117 million), which is designed to support the first three-year phase of the country's national environmental program. Regions of special emphasis include the legal Amazon, the Pantanal wetlands, and the Atlantic forest and coastal areas. An important element of the project is the strengthening of the national system of conservation units through improved protection of existing conservation areas, studies to establish new conservation units, staff training, and improved methodologies for selecting and managing conservation areas. The project also includes three measures to protect specific ecosystems.

First, the Pantanal integrated programs in the states of Mato Grosso and Mato Grosso do Sul aim to contain river pollution from agriculture, mining, and industry; protect wildlife; arrest land degradation in the ecological reserve areas of the Taquari and São Lourenco River sub-basins; devise guidelines and plans for developing and conserving the Pantanal wetlands; improve staff training; and increase environmental education of the local population. Second, the Atlantic forest integrated programs in the states of Santa Catarina, Paraná, São Paulo, Rio de Janeiro, and Espírito Santo aim to protect existing state conservation units, create additional protected areas, improve watershed protection, establish law enforcement mechanisms for pollution control and forest protection, and strengthen institutional capacity for carrying out action programs. There are also programs for environmental zoning along the Brazilian coastline, for monitoring, and for protection of endangered species. The project also contains components to strengthen federal and state environmental agencies through staff training and technical assistance, to improve technologies for environmental management, to establish a national network for environmental information and three centers for interpreting remote sensing images, and to increase environmental education.

Environmental Protection Project ($21.9 million) aims to reverse the deterioration in the lagoon by building wastewater disposal facilities, monitoring pollution, and establishing sound environmental legislation. An earlier concern about the possible effects of ocean disposal of waste and the potential movement of wastes along the coast has now been satisfactorily addressed.

Population projects can have as wide-ranging environmental benefits as projects with explicit environmental objectives. Lending for population activities is a central feature of the Bank's multisectoral approach to environment, and efforts to increase lending for population activities continue to be a priority. In fiscal 1990 lending for population, health, and nutrition (PHN) projects amounted to just over $800 million, of which some 20 to 25

Box 4–2. The Environment Management Project in Poland

Major environmental degradation problems in Poland are addressed in the Environment Management Project ($18 million). This project provides a framework for developing appropriate economic and institutional policies to address environmental problems, primarily those relating to air and water pollution and solid waste management. It will support development of an overall environmental policy and regulatory system, a program of environmental audits in the industrial sector, efforts to improve air quality in the extremely polluted Katowice-Krakow region through developing a least-cost investment strategy, and development of pilot institutions for integrated planning and management of water resources for the heavily polluted upper Vistula River basin.

---

percent was devoted to family planning. This is in line with the three-year target for PHN lending set by the Bank's president in November 1989. Moreover there is a full pipeline of projects planned for fiscal 1991–93, with 63 projects totaling $3 billion under preparation.

Although lending takes place primarily within integrated PHN projects, each year there are a small number of free-standing population projects. Special attention has been given to sector work and policy dialogue in Africa, and this is producing a greater proportion of projects in the region. Greater efforts are also being made to include local NGOs in the design and implementation of projects and to improve services to people who are hard to reach because of either geography or poverty. A larger number of social sector loans are being made, some of which directly provide for family planning, but all of which are designed to improve the quality of life of the poor and by so doing reduce the need to rely on large family size for survival.

Projects with Environmental Components

During fiscal 1990 the Bank continued to increase its efforts to build environmental objectives or ameliorative components into its projects. About 50 percent of Bank loans and credits during the year contained environmental elements (Table 4-1). The sectors in which more than half of the projects had an explicitly environmental orientation were agriculture, industry, water supply and sewerage, and urbanization. (Appendix I provides an illustrative list of projects with environmental components or objectives during fiscal 1990).

Table 4-1. Loans with Environmental Elements, by Sector, Fiscal 1990

Sector	Number of loans	Loans with environmental components	Percentage of loans with environmental components
Agriculture and rural development	55	44	80
Forestry	8	7[a]	88
Irrigation and drainage	7	7	100
Area development	9	6	67
Research and extension	10	8	80
Agroindustry	3	1	33
Other	18	15[b]	83
Transport	23	7	30
Education	21	6	29
Energy	18	8	44
Oil, gas, and coal	1	0	0
Power	17	8	47
Population, health, and nutrition	18	3	17
Urbanization	16	10	63
Water supply and sewerage	15	15[c]	100
Nonproject	14	4	29
Structural adjustment	11	4	36
Other	3	0	0
Technical assistance	11	1	9
Development finance	10	2	20
Industry	7	4	57
Small-scale enterprises	6	2	33
Public sector management	4	0	0
Telecommunications	4	1	25
Total	222	107[d]	48

a. Includes 5 free-standing loans.
b. Includes 3 free-standing loans.
c. Includes 3 free-standing loans.
d. Sector adjustment loans are included in the appropiate sector category.

In the agriculture sector projects increasingly aim directly at enhancing natural resource management and conservation. Some of the recurrent environmental elements in agriculture projects are soil conservation; improved irrigation efficiency; improved land use patterns, agroecological zoning, and titling; flood control and drainage; agroforestry; and rangeland and wildlife management. Innovative approaches to combating soil erosion and to addressing the difficult issue of managing common lands are features of two watershed development projects approved in fiscal 1990.

Support for research programs and training forms an important part of many loans, which may include such components as applied research programs for improved resource management practices or adaptive research for the development of pest and disease resistant varieties and training in proper methods of pesticide use and application.

All forestry projects now contain a strong environmental element, as illustrated by the free-standing projects described earlier. These projects reflect the Bank's shift from forestry operations primarily based on industrial concerns to those based on natural resource concerns. Recent projects incorporate previous forestry sector work, measures to ensure local participation, and a range of environmental components. Supporting the growing emphasis on forestry is an increase in Bank lending for the sector. Annual lending during fiscal 1990–94 is expected to be approximately $450 million, about triple the average during the previous four years. (The role of the Tropical Forestry Action Plan is discussed in Box 2-4.)

Energy development raises many issues of environmental concern—threats to human and natural habitats posed by hydro projects, unsustainable use of wood fuels, water and air pollution, and emission of greenhouse gases. Energy concerns often revolve around the increasing demand for power in developing countries, which aim to increase their installed generating capacity during the next decade by about 80 percent. The overwhelming bulk of this capacity will be supplied by conventional thermal (primarily coal, plus oil and gas) and hydro power. Considerable scope exists for lending to improve the environmental conditions in coal production and transport. Similarly, hydro development will continue to require strenuous efforts to ensure that resettlement and conservation of natural systems are handled properly. There is also a growing potential for using natural gas for thermal power generation and in industry. Natural gas is environmentally superior to coal, oil, or hydro sources—provided leaks are avoided—and is most appropriate in developing countries that have either their own natural gas resources or the potential to import natural gas, perhaps in liquified form. The Bank is identifying lending opportunities in this area, particularly for the very efficient and environmentally sound combined cycle units. In fiscal 1990 the Bank supported gas-based power developments through loans to India, Nigeria, and Poland.

Although less than half of the Bank's energy loans during the year contain explicit environmental objectives or components, virtually all of them contain measures to improve supply or end-use efficiency. These include rehabilitation and modernization of electricity generation, transmission and distribution systems, fuel switching, and pricing policies—all of which are aimed at reducing wasteful consumption of energy and are therefore consistent with environmental objectives. The Bank's energy

---

Box 4–3. The Energy Sector Management Assistance Program (ESMAP)

Preinvestment and other country-based activities completed or under way in the ESMAP program during fiscal 1990 continue to include numerous studies of household energy use with heavy emphasis on improving the efficiency in the production and use of biomass-based energy. Examples include assessment of photovoltaic potential in Pakistan and Yemen Arab Republic; bagasse cogeneration, minihydro, and windfarm development in India; minihydro rehabilitation in Uganda; and biomass gasifier preinvestment work in Indonesia. ESMAP work on conservation and efficiency includes a number of energy assessments and strategy studies (all of which place heavy emphasis on pricing policies) in Dominican Republic, Guatemala, Mali, Peru, and Zimbabwe; efforts to reduce power sector losses in Congo, Ecuador, Malawi, Morocco, Tanzania, and Tunisia; industrial conservation in Ghana, Senegal, Syria, and Tanzania; and improved stoves and kilns in Ghana and Rwanda.

An indication of the operational significance of ESMAP can be obtained from the facts that much of the Bank's energy sector work is conducted by ESMAP and that the $800 million of investments recommended by ESMAP have already been funded, with funding currently being arranged for a further $2.7 billion.

An important innovation during the year was the establishment of a Natural Gas Development Unit within ESMAP. It is charged with promoting natural gas use through preinvestment studies and related energy and environmental strategy work as well as through research.

---

lending operations are backed up by technical assistance through the Energy Sector Management Assistance Program (ESMAP) (Box 4-3). Energy efficiency was supported in the loan to Brazil for the Electricity Transmission and Conservation Project and in the loan to Mexico for the Transmission and Distribution Project. The former includes support for Electrobras's 1990–91 conservation program covering cogeneration and energy efficiency studies, supply of efficient light fixtures, loss-reduction equipment, and energy conservation training. The latter includes a program to improve thermal plant efficiency and availability as well as a thermal plant environmental control program. Renewable energy production was encouraged in the Energy Sector Loan to the Philippines, which includes $189 million for developing geothermal power.

Pricing energy to reflect true economic costs, including estimated environmental costs, is a recurring theme in Bank energy lending, although this is not sufficient to achieve end-use efficiency. Environmentally benign measures to increase energy efficiency are also typically justified in economic terms. However, although efficiency measures are very important, they are far from being the panacea that some parts of the environmental movement believe. The per capita consumption of energy in developing countries is very low—per capita electricity consumption is 7 percent of that in the industrial countries. Thus massive increases in energy consumption are unavoidable for even modest economic growth to occur.

Environmental issues in the industry sector have been accorded increasing attention within Bank projects. Project components range from facilities for treating effluents and installations to reduce emissions of air pollutants to the development of strategies for controlling industrial pollution. Industry projects have also included provisions for strengthening environmental guidelines, developing regulatory capacity, increasing industrial safety, and evaluating the risks of major environmental disasters.

The International Finance Corporation (IFC), although active in a number of sectors, is of course particularly heavily involved in industry (see also Box 5-1). During the fiscal year IFC projects included components to address environmental issues in a variety of areas, including chemicals, glass, paper, and vehicle manufacturing; mining; electrical power distribution; textile mills; wood processing; and food processing. Project sponsors provide information on pollution control systems, occupational health and safety procedures, the handling and disposal of dangerous chemicals, and other environmental issues. A pulp and paper project, for example, contains a mill design that minimizes pollution from liquid effluents, air emissions, and solid waste; in mining operations, environmental issues include open-pit reclamation, leakage protection, mitigation of impacts on water flows, and worker health and safety.

Water supply and sewerage projects address the need for wastewater treatment, improved drainage infrastructure, sewerage and solid waste management, and various other measures to protect water quality. A number of projects in this sector have also provided for flood control and protection measures. As in the case of energy, improved pricing—aimed not only at better financial performance, but also at more efficient water use—is standard in Bank water supply and sanitation projects.

The concentration of population in urban areas and the pivotal role that these areas play in the economies of many countries call for substantial investment in enhancing their environmental quality. Urban projects contain a variety of environmental components, including the construction and rehabilitation of urban infrastructure, the delivery of basic services, and strengthening of municipal maintenance institutions. A large proportion of environmental interventions are aimed at reducing the health hazards that result from water-related and waterborne diseases. Components in Bank projects have included provisions for storm water drainage and solid waste management, services such as garbage collection and drainage mainte-nance, improved waste disposal sites, and new sanitary landfills.

Transport projects have included components for traffic management, measures to control vehicle emissions and to mitigate pollution in ports, and criteria for road design that avoid environmental damage to forests and agricultural land. Projects in the past year also have provided technical assistance for developing institutional capacity, particularly for reviewing and evaluating the potential environmental impacts of road works.

Adjustment Lending

As noted in the 1989 progress report on the environment, sector and structural adjustment lending has begun to consciously incorporate mea-sures to protect or to enhance the management of natural resources, and sound environmental management is an explicit objective of a growing number of adjustment loans. In fiscal 1990 nine loans made as part of an adjustment program specifically addressed environmental objectives.

Within the framework of its agricultural policy, a supplementary loan for Ghana's Second Structural Adjustment Program stresses the need to improve the management of natural resources. It encourages the reform of forestry policy by improving management and price incentives to discour-age waste and to better control the volume of cutting. In addition the environmental action plan now being prepared will propose improve-ments in land management, water resource development, and coastal zone management.

Under Côte d'Ivoire's Agricultural Sector Adjustment Loan, the govern-ment will introduce reforms to improve the management of the country's natural resource base. Access to land plays an important role in the devel-opment of the agricultural sector. To support improved tenure arrange-ments, a satellite survey will take stock of current land use patterns and potential, and a pilot cadastral survey and land titling project will be implemented. Forest management is another area of concern. At the current pace of deforestation, the Ivorian forest will virtually disappear by the year 2000. Factors that have led to the mining of the native forest resources include inadequate logging policies, where short-term leases are based on land area rather than on the volume of timber harvested, and inappropriate fiscal policies for wood processing and exports. Under the loan the current system of log export quotas will be eliminated, and fiscal policies in the logging and wood processing sector will be reformed to promote the efficient use of existing resources.

The Côte d'Ivoire's Energy Sector Adjustment Loan will address envi-ronmental issues through a variety of measures that will complement those in the Agricultural Sector Adjustment Loan. As part of a national energy plan, studies are being undertaken to assess the supply of and demand for wood, both for direct consumption as fuel and as a derived demand resulting from the manufacture of charcoal. The results of these studies will form the basis for improved management of the fuelwood supply. Another measure supported by the loan will help develop the country's offshore natural gas potential, so that natural gas can replace the high-sulfur fuel currently used in electricity generation and heavy industry. This substitution will reduce the current emissions of sulfur and nitrogen oxides, carbon monoxide, and partially oxidized hydrocarbons. In turn, the use of natural gas in industry will free up supplies of butane or liquefied petroleum gas for use by urban households, thus removing some of the pressures on the fuelwood supply, particularly in the Abidjan area.

Among the main objectives of the Central African Republic's Third Structural Adjustment Program is the proper management of the country's rich forest and natural resource base. Productive management and protection of forests is critical to the well-being of rural populations as well as to the development of exports and to the nation's industrial production. Nevertheless these resources are being degraded through deforestation, poaching, land clearing, and brush fires. To strengthen environmental protection, several measures will be undertaken, including the introduction of logging permits and user fees and monitoring forestry industries to ensure their compliance with policies to protect natural resources. A forest fund will be created, financed by domestic taxes and foreign resources, to implement programs for the protection of natural resources, for forest and park management, and for reforestation. In addition the government will initiate a natural resource management program, which will include policy and institutional reforms in the forestry and wildlife sector, coupled with institutional strengthening, a forest inventory, and pilot subprojects in agroforestry and wildlife conservation. In parallel the government has requested help in preparing a Tropical Forest Action Plan to formulate a national development strategy for the forestry and wildlife sector.

One of the specific objectives of Mali's Agricultural Sector Adjustment and Investment Project is to ensure the sustainability of agricultural production through improved land management. Under Norwegian funding, several pilot schemes are now testing land management practices in specific villages and supporting a national coordinating unit, which has been created in the Ministry of Environment and Livestock to monitor and evaluate the schemes, undertake additional studies, and define a national strategy for managing resources. A future project under consideration will address these issues. Land ownership rights will be studied during the next two years to provide information on the security of land rights in various areas. Other measures will monitor the effect of pesticide and fertilizer use on water quality and will inventory the region's historic and archaeological sites.

The adjustment component in Mauritania's "hybrid" Agricultural Sector Adjustment and Investment Project supports new reforms to improve land tenure legislation and administration, while the investment component includes measures for environmental protection that will benefit some 15,000 people in farming and fishing families. Under the adjustment program the application of the land reform law will be improved to better control the rapid occupation of agricultural lands so as to increase productivity and conserve resources. The investment portion of the lending program includes provisions for reforestation through planting windbreaks, wooded zones, and orchards as well as stipulations for improved health services through training paramedical personnel, providing health equipment, and making epidemiological surveys.

In Uganda the war and generally unsettled state of internal affairs during the past 15 years have taken a heavy toll on the environment, particularly the forests. Under a Special Project Preparation Facility, the Ministry of Environmental Protection is coordinating a medium-term strategy for repairing damage to the environment and determining longer-term measures needed to conserve or renew Uganda's natural resource base.

Algeria's Economic Reform Support Loan advocates strengthening the policy and institutional framework to improve management of the environmental, population, and social dimensions of the economy. The adjustment program aims to launch the planning process necessary to articulate environmental action programs and to ensure that macroeconomic objectives are not undermined by depletion of natural resources. The agenda for economic reform also contains measures with environmentally beneficial consequences, such as programs to diversify energy sources, control water contamination, and manage water resources.

Several issues in the agriculture sector are addressed in Guyana's Second Structural Adjustment Credit. The adjustment program encourages the maintenance of research and extension services as well as water management programs. The management of forests and fisheries also receives attention.

Jamaica's Agricultural Sector Adjustment Loan identifies several areas of environmental policy that have had adverse effects on the economy. These include the pattern of land use by small farmers in hillside areas and the illegal cutting of trees in government forests—both of which are causing widespread soil erosion and as a result have increased the threats to watersheds and severity of flooding. The presence of significant pesticide residues in the soil, food, potable water, rivers, coastal waters, and fauna in

Jamaica is well documented. The government has been aware of the environmental problems caused by the improper use of chemical pesticides and has recently enacted a Pesticide Control Act. With Bank assistance the government has prepared terms of reference for a study to review the use of chemical pesticides and the policies and regulations concerning such use, including the requirements for effectively implementing the new legislation.

In addition to the nine policy-based loans outlined above, several adjustment programs have included conditions that have traditionally been sought by the Bank and that are likely to have a beneficial environmental impact. Typical components in such projects during fiscal 1990 have included the elimination or reduction of subsidies for pesticides, full-cost recovery in pricing energy or water services, improved land distribution policies and tenure arrangements, public investment in irrigation and land settlement projects, and the strengthening of social programs such as housing, health care, water supply, and sanitation.

The foregoing experience with adjustment lending activities, like the environmental strategy work on which they have typically been based, demonstrates that policy reforms need to be selected with extreme care. It is difficult to generalize about the effect of economic adjustment on the environment, and, as the September 1989 report to the Development Committee noted, policy interventions that have benign effects in one country may have exactly the opposite effects in another. Substantial, multidisciplinary efforts must therefore be made to understand the chain of causality and thus to anticipate the environmental consequences of policy interventions.

Where conflict arises between short-run macro-level adjustment policies and environmental concerns, compensatory mechanisms to avoid undesirable consequences may be built into the adjustment operation. This is consistent with the approach advocated for dealing with the social costs of adjustment. An adjustment program has a specific objective, however, and its design, and therefore its effect on the environment—or indeed on development in general—should not be considered separately from all the other macroeconomic policy, sector, and project activities occurring in any particular country. As experience during the fiscal year demonstrates, the potential environmental impact of policy reforms at the macro or sector level indicates that adjustment lending may in certain circumstances be an important means of explicitly addressing environmental objectives. However, a key characteristic of structural adjustment—rapid disbursement—may make this form of lending an inappropriate instrument when implementing complex institutional reforms that require many years of close monitoring. Hybrid lending that is comprised of an investment component and a rapidly disbursing component is now being used to achieve the dual objectives of facilitating short-run policy change and longer-term institution building.

Environmental Assessment

One of the most tangible illustrations of the Bank's efforts to incorporate environmental considerations into its lending activities was the requirement that environmental assessments be made for all projects with significant environmental impacts. The requirements are set forth in a new operational directive, which standardizes and formalizes the process for evaluating projects and specifies their categorization (category A to D, depending on their environmental importance) (Box 4-4). Classification of projects according to environmental category started midway through the fiscal year. Of the projects subject to such classification, about 20 percent

---

Box 4–4. The Environmental Assessment Operational Directive (EAOD)

The purpose of the Environmental Assessment Operational Directive (EAOD), which was issued in October 1989, is to ensure that the development options under consideration are environmentally sound and sustainable and that any environmental consequences are recognized early in the project cycle and taken into account in project design. Environmental assessments reduce the need for project conditionality because appropriate steps can be taken in advance or incorporated into project design; the process also helps avoid costs and delays in implementation due to unanticipated environmental problems. Because assessment is the borrower's responsibility, the directive plays an important role in encouraging the development of environmental capabilities and institutions in member countries. The environmental assessment process also provides a formal mechanism to address a range of issues which have been problematic in the past. These include the requirement that the borrower should undertake an appropriate process of consultation to ensure inter-agency coordination and to address the concerns of affected groups and local NGOs.

The scope, depth, and analytical techniques of an environmental assessment depend on the particular circumstances of each project. Regional and sectoral assessments, for example, can substantially reduce the work subsequently needed on specific project assessments. Regional assessments are used where a number of significant development activities with potentially cumulative impacts are planned for a reasonably localized area. They compare alternative development scenarios and recommend environmentally

were classified as category A, 40 percent as category B, and 35 percent as category C. In the IFC as well, approximately 70 projects were reviewed for their environmental impacts. About 10 percent were classified as category A, 60 percent as category B, and 30 percent as category C.

Because this is a new directive, progress and problems in its implementation need to be carefully monitored. A steering committee, consisting of representatives from the Environment Department and each regional Environment Division, has been convened to coordinate cross-regional efforts and to oversee technical activities. A training program for Bank staff on the application of the directive has been designed, and several workshops have been held throughout the Bank (see chapter 5). To support these activities, an "Environment Assessment Sourcebook" has been prepared for staff, borrowers, and consultants. It addresses issues that have posed difficulties in project implementation in the past, such as community participation, economic valuation, and institutional complexities. A draft of the

sustainable growth rates and land use patterns and policies. Sectoral assessments are used in designing sector investment programs. Alternative approaches that focus on a narrower range of issues may be acceptable for smaller projects with limited potential effects on the environment, and may be more effective in integrating environmental concerns into the borrower's planning process. Such approaches include integrated pest management programs, design criteria and pollution standards for small- or medium-scale industrial plants, and design criteria and construction supervision programs for small-scale rural works projects.

The directive delineates four categories of projects—categories A through D. Category A contains projects or components that may have diverse and significant environmental impacts and normally require a full-scale environmental assessment. The directive lists 21 kinds of projects in this category—such as dams and reservoirs, large-scale electrical transmission, and rural roads. Category B consists of projects and components that may have specific environmental impacts for which a more limited analysis or procedures would be appropriate. The EAOD describes 13 such categories, which could include many of those referred to above, but on a smaller scale, or projects such as renewable energy, public facilities, or telecommunications. In these cases design criteria or existing government standards may suffice. Category C includes projects and components that typically do not have a direct significant environmental impact, such as education, family planning, or health projects (except for the construction of facilities), and would normally not require an environmental analysis. Finally, category D consists of projects that have an environmental focus and thus do not require a separate environmental assessment.

sourcebook was ready for internal Bank review and trial implementation at the end of the fiscal year.

Since the environmental assessment is the borrower's responsibility, the ultimate success of the directive will depend on strengthening the environmental expertise within member countries. Projects with major potential impacts thus normally need to include an institutional development and training component. In addition, to help develop environmental capacity in the country, the Bank encourages the use of local expertise in the preparation of assessments and stresses the need for training courses for local specialists and consultants.

To help meet the additional burden that the implementation of the directive places on both borrowers and Bank staff, eight staff positions and $3.6 million were allocated from the Bank's contingency funds to support the environmental assessment process, with additional funding expected in the future. These resources were used by the four regions to hire qualified consultants to help identify environmental issues and the means of addressing them, prepare background studies, and develop guidelines for preparing the individual assessments. The large number of requests from country divisions reflects considerable demand for expert assistance. However, in view of the increased support for the assessment process, the Bank is optimistic that it can meet its commitments. A significant emerging issue concerns the funding requirements for assessments undertaken by borrowers; in this regard the new Technical Assistance Grant Program for the Environment is an important innovation (see chapter 6).

An important component of the assessment process is the dissemination of information. To this end the *Monthly Operational Summary* will now provide more detailed information on the categorization of projects according to their expected environmental impact as well as on important environmental issues and proposed actions.

Monitoring and Evaluation

All projects are routinely monitored during implementation by the staff responsible for them. After completion, projects are then evaluated by an independent department to identify problems and suggest improvements for future projects.

Project Monitoring

During the past year Bank staff have expended considerable effort supervising a number of projects approved in earlier years, some of which have been highly controversial. This supervision has been concerned with various issues, such as the need to implement adequate measures to protect the environment and to mitigate the potential negative effects of certain investments on local populations.

BOTSWANA LIVESTOCK. The Bank's livestock projects in Botswana, such as the National Land Management and Livestock Project, have aimed to encourage and support the government's efforts to formulate and implement policies to reduce overstocking and land degradation. The Bank's support for the latest of these projects is based on the need to replace the uncontrolled exploitation of communal grazing lands with a more rational approach. Nevertheless the projects have attracted criticism on issues such as overgrazing; negative economic returns, including diversion of public funds as subsidies; biases in providing credit to large-scale commercial ranches rather than to small-scale breeders; and the heavy toll on wildlife from fencing or "veterinary cordons." However, much of the criticism has been based on inaccurate information. For example, the Bank has not financed cordon fencing and has in fact urged that the fencing policy be reviewed in the national conservation strategy. The project has profited from the lessons of the past, and several elements designed to address previous problems in implementation and to build national capacity for land and wildlife management have been included, such as the gazetting of additional wildlife management areas. In addition the concept of rational land-use planning (such as zoning, allocation, and monitoring), originally intended for only four of the districts, has been adopted throughout the country.

NARMADA RIVER BASIN. In 1985 the World Bank approved a loan and credit to support the construction of the Sardar Sarovar dam in India and a credit for its associated irrigation and drainage system. The dam and associated works form part of the government's long-term development program for the Narmada River Basin. As originally envisaged by Indian planners (Narmada Water Disputes Tribunal NWDT), four large dams and numerous smaller dams would be constructed along the Narmada River during the next half century or so. Sardar Sarovar, the first of these dams, is designed to bring irrigation, electricity, and drinking water to millions of people in the drought-prone state of Gujarat in western India and electricity to Madhya Pradesh and Maharashtra. The development of the Narmada River Basin—and the Sardar Sarovar dam in particular—have been widely criticized by both local and international NGOs, primarily because of environmental and resettlement concerns.

In the Sardar Sarovar project, international attention has focused on three long-standing concerns: economic viability, resettlement, and the inundation of forest land. The Japanese decision in May 1990 to suspend a financial commitment for the current fiscal year for turbines and generators has further underscored these issues.

A number of Indian and foreign NGOs raised the economic viability of the Sardar Sarovar Dam as an issue during 1988–89. Some of their calculations suggested that the rate of return would be negative and that the project would not be economically viable. Bank staff reviewed the published report of the critics, taking into account the assumptions and calculations made in the original economic analysis in 1984–85 as well as an almost two-year delay in project start-up, the lower-than-projected costs of the dam (after allowing for inflation), the higher-than-projected resettlement and environmental costs, the environmental benefits previously not considered, and the higher electric power benefits. The staff concluded that the original economic rate of return of about 12 percent was still correct.

The resettlement issue has been the main focus of attention by critics. The original NWDT award stipulated, among other things, a resettlement policy that included allocation of irrigated land in Gujarat for resettling people affected by the Sardar Sarovar dam. In the early stages of the project there were problems regarding availability of irrigated land and the rights of the people to be displaced—particularly in exercising their options for resettlement packages and preferences for relocation. Because of these problems, concerned NGOs in India took up the cause of the "oustees," as the displaced people are called, and agitated for policy reform. These efforts helped focus attention on the problems and led to reform and improved implementation of the resettlement and rehabilitation programs.

All three affected states—Gujarat, Madhya Pradesh, and Maharashtra—have now adopted new policies for resettlement and rehabilitation. The process of identifying alternative agricultural land and resettlement sites is well under way. In Gujarat some 14 NGOs are now participating in various aspects of resettlement and rehabilitation, including the committee that is facilitating the purchase of private land by people affected by the project. To date there is no shortage of alternative land for resettlement.

Some claim that the Sardar Sarovar dam will inundate forest areas. The fact is that very little "forest" (in the ecological sense) is at stake, since the areas of inundation designated "forestland" are virtually devoid of trees or other vegetation. Specific studies and work programs are under way on fisheries, catchment treatment, and wildlife (flora and fauna). Concerns about archaeological sites and basin-wide environmental management are also receiving additional attention.

SINGRAULI. The availability of large coal reserves surrounding the Rihand reservoir makes the Singrauli area a major center of power generation in north central India. The area has attracted considerable industrial development since the 1950s, both public and private. The Bank's involvement in developing the Singrauli area has consisted of two IDA credits for thermal power development, one IBRD loan for coal development, and one for power transmission, as well as a recent urban renewal component for the town of Shaktinagar. Virtually all of these projects are completed. The Singrauli development has been criticized by both Indian and international NGOs for air and water pollution hazards, for the working conditions in some coal mines, for the lack of urban planning, and for the manner in which inhabitants have been relocated (sometimes more than once) before adequate provisions for managing the resettlement were in place. The Bank's analysis agrees with many of these criticisms.

Singrauli is a classic example of cumulative environmental impact, both physical and social. This cumulative impact occurs when several development projects are implemented without properly assessing their environmental impacts. The choice for the Bank in such circumstances is between stepping aside, on the grounds that the projects it has helped finance are closed (or almost closed), or offering to help address the area's problems. In Singrauli it chose the latter course of action. An environmental impact assessment study, financed under the Bank's Singrauli Thermal II project, evaluated these wider concerns. The assessment was done for the government of India and the National Thermal Power Corporation by independent consultants. To address the serious environmental degradation of the Singrauli area, separate interventions are being considered—either as part of existing projects in the states bordering Singrauli or as components in new projects. Project components could include the strengthening of the institutional framework for environmental management and rehabilitation, development of improved regional planning capacities, reforestation, resettlement and rehabilitation, and air and water pollution control, as well as measures to deal with social effects.

KEDUNG OMBO. This project in Indonesia is an example of the problems that can occur during the shift toward stronger environmental policies. It is a classic hydroelectric and irrigation dam development, prepared in 1984 and initiated in 1985. The reservoir was filled in 1989, and disbursements will be completed in 1991 or 1992.

The overriding issue, as in the case of most similar investments, has been compensating and resettling more than 4,000 families in the 20 villages that were submerged. Because of the high population densities in areas around the future reservoir and the low productivity of upland areas nearby, the government of Indonesia favored resettlement elsewhere through transmigration. Resistance to these plans by a small minority of the affected population then led to a revised plan to provide those families with opportunities to settle nearby, with constraints on land clearance to ensure protection of the dam watershed. This revised plan included features such as environmental protection (for a greenbelt and littoral zones), development of alternative resources (fish stocking of the reservoir), and health and education facilities, together with a monitoring program.

For a variety of reasons, including less-than-satisfactory supervision by the Bank and often-difficult negotiations between the government and the affected residents, this plan was not implemented before the dam was filled. The new sequence of environmental assessment and early implementation of resettlement plans should help avoid a recurrence of such problems in future projects. However, it is also clear from this experience that affected communities must be consulted and involved in planning to win their cooperation in resettlement programs.

CARAJAS. The Carajas Iron Ore project formed part of Brazil's regional plans for developing mining and mining-related sectors in eastern Amazonia. The project was carried out by the Companhia Vale do Rio Doce (CVRD). The CVRD has executed the project with due care to environmental considerations and has incurred costs of more than $60 million for protecting the environment in the project area, plus more than $12 million for protecting the Amerindian population.

However, with government fiscal incentives, 4 pig iron smelters have been established and 13 more are planned along the rail line (outside of the CVRD's concession), using charcoal as the principal source of energy. This is a cause of considerable concern, as it may lead to large-scale deforestation. In response, the Bank and the Brazilian government, with financial support from the German government through the ESMAP program, will study alternative energy options for the pig iron smelters, review relevant government pricing and fiscal policies, and assess the economics of the pig iron smelters. The main mission is expected to take place by November 1990.

POLONOROESTE. In 1980, in recognition of the growing socioeconomic problems caused by accelerating migration to Rondonia and Mato Grosso in the Amazon Basin, the Brazilian government launched a program of major investments in these Northwest agricultural frontier areas. The Integrated Development Program for Northwest Brazil (Polonoroeste) aimed to absorb the human influx in an orderly and sustainable manner. The main parts of the program were Bank financing to pave a main federal highway, coupled with construction of feeder roads to that highway; three agricultural projects designated to settle migrants in areas with the best soils; and a health improvement project. In contrast to earlier government initiatives, environmental considerations did play an important part in the design of Polonoroeste, including the creation and protection of forest and Amerindian reserves and the establishment of sustainable tree crop production in previously deforested areas.

There have been numerous problems in implementing these projects. Important differences between the original planning assumptions and implementation were found, so the Bank and the government agreed to limit new settlements and infrastructure investment, and efforts on both the institutional and technical fronts were intensified. The objective of widely introducing permanent tree crops in place of subsistence slash-and-burn cultivation has not been fully achieved, and the rates of migration and deforestation continued to be high.

However, Polonoroeste's weaknesses have tended to mask some of its significant accomplishments. Most targets have now been met, including the establishment of conservation units and the demarcation of Amerindian areas, and key institutions have been created or strengthened. Polonoroeste has also been responsible for the development of new technical knowledge, which has facilitated a major agroecological zoning effort and the assessment of the environmental policy framework and has fostered a growing political and public commitment to preserve the Amazon's remaining natural resources. Looking to the future, the environmental policy and incentive framework needs to be further improved and the state planning and implementation capacity strengthened. These issues are to be addressed under the proposed Rondonia Natural Resources Management Project currently being prepared. This project would also address the need to further strengthen the state's environmental protection, monitoring, and enforcement capacity to reduce the rate of forest clearing, unauthorized mining, squatting and illegal invasions of conservation units and Amerindian reserves.

LESSONS FOR THE FUTURE. The above examples have shown that the Bank must ensure that the lessons of past problems are quickly reflected in future policy adjustments. Although paying closer attention to the environmental aspects of projects—as exemplified by the introduction of a more systematic environmental assessment process—should reduce such problems in the future, project monitoring is likely, on balance, to place much greater demands on staff resources than in the past. The growing number of free-standing environmental projects and environmental components has required heavy inputs from Bank staff in the identification and preparation stages, and this will shortly have to be matched by a substantial increase in monitoring and supervision efforts—by both the Bank and its borrowers.

The 1987 report to the Development Committee noted that proper implementation of the environmental components of projects has always been a problem. Difficulties arise because of the nature of environmental issues: in some cases, since externalities tend to be a distinguishing characteristic of environmental problems, the borrower or executing agency can be expected not to perceive the loan conditions to be in its own self-interest; in other cases, implementation requires attention to concerns arising in a variety of sectors, making it necessary to rely on time-consuming multidisciplinary analysis. Failure to strengthen the supervision capacity of both the Bank and the borrower means that loan conditions may not be complied with and that the ultimate objectives of the major shift in emphasis toward environmental concerns in project preparation will not be realized. Therefore a priority will be to assist borrowers in building the institutional capability for environmental monitoring and regulation.

Operations Evaluation

As in previous years, the Bank's Operations Evaluation Department (OED) addressed environmental issues in its review of all project completion reports and its own performance audit work. The *Annual Review of Evaluation Results for 1988,* published during the year, identified the principal determinants of sustainable economic development, with special reference to the management of natural resources. It presents several lessons from Bank experience as well as recommendations for future actions. Some of the most important ones are related to the significant role of macroeconomic performance and management in attaining sustainable development. The Bank should increase its attention to institutional issues, review the environmental implications in public expenditure and investment reviews, and generally incorporate environmental concerns into macroeconomic policy and procedures.

OED is also conducting three special studies specifically concerned with the environmental dimensions and effects of Bank activity. These studies examine the environmental aspects and consequences of selected Bank-supported projects in Brazil, natural resource management in Bolivia and Nepal, and the Bank's experience with involuntary resettlement. The Brazil study assesses how the Bank has perceived and dealt with physical and human environmental issues in several large infrastructure, productive sector, and environmental protection operations implemented during the past two decades. The questions examined range from deforestation, the loss of biodiversity, and the protection of tribal populations in the eastern and western parts of the tropical Amazon region, to forced resettlement and water resource use in the semi-arid northeast, and pollution control and urban environmental management in the heavily industrial state of Sao Paulo. All field work, which was carried out jointly with representatives of the Brazilian government, has been completed, and three of the four reports are available in draft form. An overview report will be presented to the Board during fiscal 1991.

The natural resource management study of Nepal has also been largely completed. This study examines how the use and administration of natural resources has been treated in Bank country policy dialogue and economic and sector work, as well as in the entire range of externally financed investment projects, during the past 25 years. A similar exercise will be undertaken for Bolivia, and the corresponding report is also expected to be released during fiscal 1991.

The third major ongoing environmental study concerns the effect of involuntary resettlement in Bank-assisted hydropower and agricultural projects. Its specific objectives are to determine the extent to which resettlement has been successfully undertaken, including the types of agricultural development strategies and institutional mechanisms employed and their effect on beneficiary incomes and living standards, local labor markets, host populations, and the physical environment. The study focuses on Asia, where the largest number of Bank operations involving involuntary resettlement have been implemented to date, although one or more African cases may also be examined. Socioeconomic surveys of affected populations have been completed in Thailand and are presently being carried out in India. A report is expected to be issued within a year.

Toward the end of fiscal 1990 OED also began a study of the Bank's experience in forestry. The study will examine relevant experience in project and sector work and is meant to help Bank operational staff design and implement forestry projects or programs. The environment will be a central theme of the study, which will highlight appropriate institutional, economic, technical, and social issues.

5. Organization of the Bank's Environmental Work

Organizational Responsibilities and Staffing

Environmental work is becoming increasingly integrated into the Bank's economic and sector work and lending operations. The bulk of this work is undertaken by the Country Departments. The units charged with responsibility for environmental policy are the Environment Department, located in the Policy, Research, and External Affairs Senior Vice Presidency (PRE), and four Environment Divisions, one in the Technical Department of each of the four Regional Offices. The Environment Department, comprised of 24 higher-level staff and about 8 consultants, conducts policy and research functions in technical, economic, and social areas; supplies operational support to the regions in certain specialized areas; and provides training for staff. It has also been heavily involved in external relations work. The regional Environment Divisions, which together contain 30 higher-level staff and about 15 consultants, provide expertise and operational support and are responsible for monitoring and ensuring the soundness of Bank projects throughout the project cycle. The financial resources of the environmental units in fiscal 1990 are summarized in Annex II. The data demonstrate the direct support from a number of governments, in some cases through secondment of staff, as well as some funding from the UNDP.

The number of people employed by the environmental units is a subject of some interest outside the Bank and is often taken as an indication of the importance placed on the subject by Bank management. It is of course a very misleading indicator. Although the size of the environmental units has increased tenfold since before the Bank's reorganization in July 1987, this is but the tip of the iceberg. Most important to the integration of environmental concerns into the Bank's daily activities is the large number of Bank staff working entirely or partly on environmental matters. They are now to be found throughout the Operations complex, in PRE, and among Legal, Finance, and Operations Evaluation staff. The process of integrating environmental concerns into the whole range of Bank operations is moving rapidly, as is illustrated by the large number of environmental strategy activities, free-standing projects, project components, and adjustment lending operations described in this report and by the fact that environmental and natural resource management specialists are increasingly being recruited by country departments to work exclusively on environmental sector work and projects. In addition the IFC has recently introduced new environmental procedures and is integrating environmental issues into its operations (Box 5-1).

As environmental work becomes integrated into all aspects of the Bank's operations, the regional divisions are becoming increasingly involved in reviewing environmental strategy as well as project-related activities. The regional divisions perform many of the functions that, at the central level, are carried out by the Environment Department, including staff training. Close relationships are maintained between the Environment Department and the regional divisions, each of which has played a major role in formulating policy and guidelines. Examples include background work for the Global Environmental Facility, development of a policy on pesticides, and preparation of the guidelines to be used with the Environmental Assessment Operational Directive (EAOD).

A variety of skills are employed in the regional environmental units, and the composition of the skills has changed to emphasize ecology, sociology or anthropology, and environmental engineering. These skills are also present in the Environment Department, but economics is much more significant there and accounts for one quarter of the staff. The Environment Department also employs four higher-level staff in its geographic information systems unit. Since environmental work often requires intimate knowledge of a particular location, consultants are, and will continue to be, heavily relied on. For the bulk of the work, however, skills already present in the Bank can be successfully adapted to formulate policies and to prepare and supervise projects.

Staff Training

Training staff on environmental matters is a crucial element in integrating environmental concerns into the work of the Bank. It can demonstrate to staff both the relevance of the skills they already possess and the areas in which they need to call on specialized assistance. Training courses on environmental issues—conducted by staff from the Environment Department, other sector departments in PRE, and the regional Environment Divisions as well as by consultants—has continued at a rapid pace, and about 20 major seminars (one-half to two-and-a-half days long) were conducted during the year. In addition about 100 informal seminars have taken

Box 5-1. The International Finance Corporation (IFC)

IFC policy dictates that all projects in which it invests are to be consistent with the spirit and intent of appropriate World Bank environmental guidelines and policies and in compliance with the environmental requirements of the host country. Last year the position of environmental advisor was established in the Engineering Department to help implement this policy. The IFC's environmental management capability was strengthened further in fiscal 1990 when it adopted its procedure for environmental review of projects.

The IFC procedures were developed to ensure that all prospective projects undergo an environmental review as part of project appraisal. The procedure covers not only environmental issues but also socioeconomic concerns, resettlement issues, occupational health and safety, major hazard analysis, and risk to life and property. It is consistent with the intent of the Bank's Environmental Assessment Operational Directive (EAOD), which defines the environmental assessment process to be applied to IBRD and IDA loans and credits, and is designed to ensure that all IFC projects conform fully to the same standards. Although the IFC procedures rely on Bank guidelines and overall policy, its review process is adapted to the nature of IFC investments in the private sector.

The definitions of project categories are similar—but not identical—to those used by the Bank (see Box 4-4). In addition to the 7 IFC projects falling under category A and 67 under category B, 5 projects were required to complete an additional major hazard assessment, as outlined in the World Bank guidelines "Techniques for Assessing Industrial Hazards." Finally, 36 projects, primarily those associated with the development of capital markets, required no environmental review and therefore came under category C.

The IFC also plans to promote and finance private sector production of environment goods and services in developing countries. In fiscal 1990 it initiated several country studies aimed at defining a more active role for itself in this area. As government agencies and private companies become more aware of their environmental obligations and more responsible in living up to them, shortages of the necessary goods and services can become the main constraints on progress. This in turn can lead to commercially viable and economically attractive opportunities in which the IFC can provide investment and technical services. Possible activities include hazardous waste treatment and disposal, solid waste management, industrial and municipal wastewater treatment, potable water treatment and distribution, the manufacture of pollution control equipment and monitoring instrumentation, and the provision of consulting, engineering, and laboratory services.

place. A vast range of topics has been covered, typically on an ad hoc basis in response to interest expressed by Bank staff. However, two sets of training courses that were introduced during the fiscal year—environmental analysis for country and sector economists and environmental assessments training project task managers—were aimed at key groups of staff and will continue during the next few years.

The course for economists acquaints them with the main issues related to environment and development and with the Bank's approach to these issues. It covers the links between macroeconomic and sectoral policies, the role and limitations of cost-benefit analysis, the use of regulations and incentives, and issues related to sustainability and limits to growth. Case studies demonstrate that environmental issues are a legitimate concern of country and sector economists, not only because environmental degradation is increasingly of macroeconomic importance in threatening economic growth, but also because economic instruments are indispensable means of achieving environmental objectives. The two-day course was given to the staff of the Africa and the Europe, Middle East, and North Africa Regions during the year.

Training staff to implement the EAOD was a major exercise in fiscal 1990. Following a series of introductory seminars on environmental assessment to familiarize Bank staff with the requirements of the new directive, a more comprehensive series of seminars was developed. A program of two-day seminars covers key procedures, initial evaluation, social assessment, and implementation issues. The seminars use case studies and emphasize practical guidance, such as preparation of terms of reference, monitoring and supervision, and ways to ensure public participation in the assessment process. The NGO community has been consulted about the directive, and a workshop on this and other issues was held with African NGOs at the Bank.

6. Special Funding Arrangements

A prime objective of both the Bank and its member countries is to develop policies and projects that meet both economic and environmental criteria. The experience of environmental strategy work increasingly demonstrates that there are many such opportunities, and in these cases additional funding above and beyond existing channels is often unnecessary. But sometimes tradeoffs remain. For example, while many developing countries have already taken steps to improve the management of their natural resources, urgent short-term needs constrain the ability of some of them to undertake costly conservation measures. This is often compounded by the relatively high discount rates of decisionmakers and by uncertainty about the economic and physical consequences of environmental degradation. When environmental problems and their consequences cross national boundaries, there is the further complication of deciding who should bear the cost of protecting the environment. Increasing public awareness of the global and regional effects of a number of environmental problems—such as depletion of the ozone layer, climate change, marine pollution, and species extinction—has led to negotiations, mainly among industrial countries, about the way in which such problems might be addressed. Various initiatives have emerged in recent years, including a new Global Environmental Facility, debt-for-nature swaps, and increased technical assistance funding.

Global Environmental Facility

The new set of global environmental problems tend to reflect the growing physical and economic interdependence among nations. Although primary responsibility for these problems continues to rest with the industrial countries, developing countries will increasingly contribute to global air and water pollution as their economies expand.

A central concern in addressing global issues will continue to be the question of how best to assist developing countries to take measures to protect the "global commons." Additional concessionary funding may be required where the country bears the costs for environmental protection, but where the benefits accrue to the global community. The French government raised this issue at the 1989 Development Committee discussions, and the Bank was asked to investigate the feasibility of a special fund to finance the investments required.

Bank staff subsequently met with potential donor governments and with colleagues in UNEP and the UNDP early in 1990. In light of these discussions, a paper was presented to the Development Committee in May 1990 on the establishment of a Global Environmental Facility. The facility would fund pilot and experimental programs in four areas of global environmental intervention: protection of the ozone layer, reduction in greenhouse gas emissions that cause global warming, protection of biodiversity, and protection of international water resources. The facility would assist governments both to develop cost-effective ways to implement programs that address these global problems and to build the institutional capacities to support such programs.

The paper proposed that such a fund be established on a pilot basis for three years and be located in the Bank. UNEP and the UNDP would be partners in a tripartite arrangement, so that the necessary actions would involve each agency according to its mandate and comparative advantage. The proposal recognized that although fundamental scientific and technological uncertainties about global environmental trends will persist, there are also many actions that can be taken now, at modest cost, to reduce potential impacts. The Bank argued that operating such a pilot fund would provide important experience about the costs, feasibility, and policies appropriate for concerted international action.

The Development Committee concluded that efforts to develop proposals for a pilot funding mechanism should continue, taking into account the Bank's existing programs. The Bank was urged to reinforce and expand its current environmental programs and thus help developing countries to achieve the same objective according to their priorities. The Bank was directed to proceed with this work expeditiously in consultation with interested parties and in close collaboration with UNEP and the UNDP. Members underlined the need for sufficient flexibility to attract as wide support as possible.

In early June, in Paris, the Bank consulted further with the interested parties (including donor and nondonor countries) about how such a facility might operate and what it might cover. The original proposal had listed four areas of possible coverage, and there was a detailed discussion on how a global fund might be applied to various categories of action in these areas, particularly where a country would otherwise have no incentive to give priority to such action. Participants showed growing support for the pilot concept and a great deal of interest in the way in which the tripartite arrangement between the Bank, UNEP, and the UNDP would work in practice.

A related aspect of international cooperation on such matters of common concern is the protection of the ozone layer. An intergovernmental commitment existed under the 1987 Montreal Protocol to phase out the use of harmful substances, such as CFCs. Although the funding mechanism foreshadowed in the protocol had not previously been defined, a ministerial meeting of the parties to the Montreal Protocol met in London in June 1990 to resolve this question and to adopt an accelerated timetable for meeting the commitments agreed to in the protocol.

The London meeting, which the Bank attended as an observer, achieved consensus on these points, and agreement was reached to establish a fund of at least $160 million over three years. The parties to the protocol set up an executive committee to oversee these arrangements. The Bank has been asked to administer and manage this fund, which will finance the incremental costs incurred by developing countries in addressing global environmental concerns.

Fiscal 1990 therefore closed on a positive note with respect to global environmental issues. There was tangible evidence of the international community's wish to move from discussing general principles to implementing programs of action, not only in the developing countries, but also throughout the industrial world. The new impetus given by the parties to the Montreal Protocol to the action required in one key area will spill over into others, partly because CFCs have also been a significant component of the total contribution to the greenhouse effect and partly because the new principle of collective insurance against severe global disruption is beginning to emerge. The Bank's initiative was based on this principle and on the need to ensure that the programs for environmental actions developed with borrowing countries did not leave out the global dimension and the need for fresh resource transfers to take it into account.

Debt for Nature

Another way to transfer resources to developing countries to improve the environment is through debt-for-nature swaps. The Bank has not been directly involved in these transactions but has been developing contacts with the main NGOs involved. In the report of the Executive Directors on IDA-9, donors urged the International Development Association (IDA) to "play a catalytic role in facilitating debt-for-nature transactions in support of sustainable development." As a result a policy paper discussing possible Bank support for this activity was prepared for the Board and approved by it in May 1990.

Since July 1987, 10 debt-for-nature transactions have been arranged in 7 countries, including Bolivia, Costa Rica, Ecuador, Madagascar, the Philippines, Poland, and Zambia. The face value of the debt involved in these swaps has been about $84 million. Although NGOs have been involved in all of these transactions, funding has also come from Dutch, Swedish, German, and US governments, as well as from a commercial bank that in one case donated rather than sold its claim.

The objectives of debt-for-nature transactions are consonant with the Bank's expanding involvement in, and support for, increasing environmental activities and reducing debt burdens. Although the Bank will not directly finance such transactions, there are a number of ways in which it might facilitate transactions that are a natural outgrowth of its lending and policy dialogue and are in line with its role as a development institution.

Some of the mechanisms include:

- Working with governments through policy dialogue and economic and sector analysis to create macroeconomic environmental—and possibly regulatory—frameworks that would facilitate these transactions
- Helping to mobilize resources for debt-for-nature transactions where they are a part of a larger program of environmental action or debt reduction in which the Bank has been involved
- Providing information to governments on potential debt-for-nature opportunities and possibly bringing interested governments, commercial banks, and NGOs together
- Providing lending operations coordinated or cofinanced with debt-for-nature transactions that would improve the effectiveness or sustainability of environmental actions; for adjustment loans with environmental components, a portion of such loans may be set aside for debt and debt service reduction within the guidelines of such operations.

Bank efforts to facilitate debt-for-nature transactions are apt to be staff intensive and should not be considered a separate program of special emphasis. Staff are encouraged, however, to take advantage of opportunities that arise in the course of the Bank's ongoing work to support other agencies active in this field.

Technical Assistance

In previous years the financing of environmental projects has been constrained by inadequate funds for project preparation. To help the formulation of viable environmental investment programs and policies, several bilateral donors have recently provided increased grants for technical assistance. In mid-1989 the Bank set up a Technical Assistance Grant Program for the Environment, and, after reviewing Bank proposals for the utilization of such funds, the Japanese government formally approved a grant of $16.6 million for this purpose. Of the total, $5 million was allocated for 13 IDA projects and programs, and the remaining $11.6 million was for 22 such activities in the IBRD. The program is expected to continue in future years.

The grants in fiscal 1990 financed a broad spectrum of technical assistance activities, ranging in size and sectoral content from the National Forestry Development Project in Guinea-Bissau ($140,000) to the Environment and Natural Resources Management Sector Adjustment Loan to the Philippines ($1 million). A grant is supporting the preparation of a Wildlife Management and Environmental Conservation Project in Zimbabwe, which aims to enhance government strategy for wildlife and habitat protection, to strengthen opportunities for generating income from wildlife, to encourage the integration of wildlife utilization with other land uses, and to carry out studies of the tourism subsector in the country. Another grant was approved for the preparation of the Punjab Urban Environment Protection Project in Pakistan, which addresses the decline in urban environmental quality, especially the problems posed by water pollution and hazardous wastes. So far a small proportion of the funding has been used specifically for environmental assessment as defined in the EAOD, but this is expected to become an increasingly important element of the program in the future.

In addition to the Japanese grant, the Bank has now received commitments for technical assistance in environmental areas from Canada ($4.5 million), Denmark ($3 million), Finland ($1.5 million), France ($1.2 million), Norway ($2 million), and Sweden ($5 million). Except for the Norwegian grant, these contributions are tied to the procurement of goods and services from the respective donors.

7. The World Bank and the International Community

External Relations

The main links that have been built up with the international community fall into three categories. First, there are the specialist groupings of international agencies and bilateral aid donors, such as the Committee of International Development Institutions on the Environment, the OECD/DAC Ad Hoc Working Group on the Environment, and the regular meetings of bodies such as UNEP and the International Union on Conservation of Nature and Natural Resources (IUCN), as well as the liaison groups that have been set up by UNEP to improve coordination within the UN family, such as the Designated Officials on Environmental Matters and the Ecosystem Co-ordinating Group. This is not an exhaustive list, but these groupings represent the main focus of professional contact with colleagues engaged in parallel efforts. Special working-level liaison with the UNDP is maintained through an annual one-day conference.

The second category of contact is the environmental NGOs. They are now very numerous and represent a wide spectrum of citizen interest groups, as well as activist lobbies with more closely defined agendas. The links with these groups are an important feature of the Bank's environmental strategy. Deliberate efforts have been made to increase the flow of information to NGOs and to consult with them on policy issues, such as the Global Environmental Facility and the implementation of the Environmental Assessment Operational Directive (EAOD).

Finally, there are the many special events that have an environmental theme—symposiums on key resources such as energy and water; gatherings of scientists, consulting engineers, officials, and parliamentarians; and specialized groupings that the Bank itself has convened or sponsored, such as environmental economists, experts on natural disasters, and advisers on industrial risk management. In this category are the series of meetings and conferences that have been called in various regions to follow up on the Bruntland Report, as the book *Our Common Future* has come to be known.

Senior managers participated in the conference on Global Environment and Human Response towards Sustainable Development in Tokyo and in the European Ministers' Conference in Bergen, Norway, on Action for a Common Future. The most important special event will be the UN Conference on Environment and Development (UNCED), which will be held in Brazil in 1992 to focus on how to integrate environmental factors into the process of social and economic development. The Bank will help prepare for the conference, and close links have already been established with the UNCED secretariat. The subject of the 1992 *World Development Report* will be the environment, and publication will coincide with the final preparations for that conference.

In addition to participation in international meetings and conferences, the Bank has a general outreach program that targets academic centers and the international media, which now devotes a large amount of space to the interface between the environment and development. Senior environmental staff regularly give in-depth media interviews in Washington, D.C., and in other countries. These efforts are supplemented by circulation of the Bank's increasing output of published material on the environment.

These publications, listed in the bibliography, cover a wide range of subjects and include research papers, technical books, and periodic progress reports to the Development Committee. In addition the bimonthly newsletter, "Environment Bulletin," has a circulation of 12,000 copies— 3,000 of which go to NGOs. During the year some 16 books on environmental issues were published, several of which were among the Bank's most widely distributed publications. Notable among these were *Conserving the World's Biological Diversity, Environmental Management and Economic Development, People and Trees: The Role of Social Forestry in Sustainable Development, Striking a Balance: The Environmental Challenge of Development, The Safe Disposal of Hazardous Wastes,* and *Vetiver Grass: The Hedge against Erosion.*

Some of the most substantive links with other agencies and NGOs during the past year have been developed through dealing with specific issues, such as the EAOD and the TFAP, as well as through substantive discussions about environmental policies. Complementing the training activities for government staff (described below), special efforts are being made to bring indigenous NGOs into the process of environmental assessment. For example, this topic was covered during the workshop for African NGOs, and the National Wildlife Federation and the Osborne Center led a Bank symposium on local users and uses of tropical rainforests.

The Environmental Program for the Mediterranean (EPM), released during the year, was a product of close collaboration between the Bank, the European Investment Bank (EIB), the European Community, the UNDP, and UNEP. The conference in Paris of Mediterranean countries to review the draft report was a model of governmental and interagency cooperation. The important topic of biodiversity has also been one in which the Bank has collaborated fruitfully with other agencies and NGOs. It participated in the successful Consultative Meeting on Conservation of Critical Ecosystems and Economic Development, held in Bangkok in late 1989. Sponsored by the IUCN, USAID, UNEP, the WRI, the WWF, and the Bank, the meeting surveyed the views of approximately 15 Asian governments on biodiversity to help formulate priorities and make recommendations for investment funding.

External Training: The Economic Development Institute

The Bank's Economic Development Institute (EDI), which runs training courses and seminars for officials from developing countries, has for many years implicitly featured environmental concerns in its activities. Now, however, the environment has even more prominence in its courses. EDI's general approach is to incorporate environmental concerns into existing programs. In addition, in fiscal 1990, EDI ran 10 national workshops jointly with Bank operational staff on environmental assessment. Workshops in North Africa and Latin America covered the Bank's new requirements, national environmental laws and regulations applicable to specific types of investment, and ways by which countries should routinely introduce environmental assessments in project preparation activities.

EDI seminars on infrastructure, irrigation, and public health have always examined the environmental aspects of water resource management. However, a more coherent approach to water resource development has recently been adopted, as exemplified by the seminars on integrated water resource development conducted in Malaysia and Thailand. Similarly, regional energy policy and planning seminars are increasingly taking the environment as a central theme.

Other important activities include EDI's collaboration with the Swedish International Development Agency in helping to create an environmental education and training network among selected universities in Africa. This effort is being made in response to a proposal from the African Ministers Conference on the Environment. Recommendations are now being studied by the universities concerned, and individual proposals will be submitted to donor agencies. EDI expects to play a significant role in this long-term program.

Finally, EDI is also devoting increasing attention to the subject of managing tropical rainforests. Most of the effort is currently under way in Brazil, where EDI supports the training center of the superintendency for the development of the center-west region of the country. A series of annual senior policy seminars on tropical forestry and management is scheduled to begin in 1991, initially for the countries of the Amazon basin.

8. Progress and Prospects

Response to the 1989 Agenda

Overall the Bank has made considerable progress during the past fiscal year in responding to the agenda set out in the September 1989 report to the Development Committee and in addressing the five priority environmental problems identified at the beginning of this report.

Environmental issues are beginning to be treated more systematically in country economic work, but much more still needs to be done. The foundation for achieving this objective rests on the design of an ambitious training program in environmental issues for all country and sector economists. Actual training courses began toward the end of the fiscal year.

This year showed a considerable increase in the number of free-standing environmental loans approved by the Board. Lending in this category increased from 2 projects in fiscal 1989 to 11 in fiscal 1990. This progress is expected to continue, with 45 projects anticipated for fiscal 1991–93.

Population lending during the fiscal year met the targets established, and the pipeline for future projects shows an even greater increase. This is important because of the link with future pressures on the environment—a link that has been explicitly recognized by the Bank.

These trends have greatly increased the scope for innovation and fresh analysis of policy options for operations at the country level, and formal environmental research programs are now evolving in both the Sector Policy and Research and the Development Economics Vice Presidencies. Joint research activities are also being prepared by the Environment and the Country Economics Departments on environmental policy interventions and on sustainability—both of which are necessary to properly integrate environmental concerns into macroeconomic work.

Procedures to ensure that environmental considerations are properly addressed in the Bank's projects are working well. The Environmental Assessment Operational Directive (EAOD) is being implemented, and Bank staff and borrowers are being trained in its use. Although designed to avoid adding to the cost and time of project implementation in future years, the procedure is complex and time consuming and places a heavy burden on staff and borrowers. Potentially more serious is the huge monitoring and supervision load that is beginning to emerge. The substantial increase in the environmental elements of projects, combined with the inherent complexities in implementing them, indicate that steps need to be taken now to prepare for the increased effort that will be required. Building up the institutional capacity in borrowing countries for project monitoring, environmental regulation, and policy reform aimed at environmental objectives will be a priority. Failure to do so may mean that the gains made so far in improving the Bank's environmental project work will prove to have been illusory.

The Bank has contributed actively to ongoing international efforts on the emerging environmental problems of global consequence. In particular it has played a central role in responding to increasing donor interest in the rationale and feasibility of a new global environmental fund.

The Bank continues to attach great importance to improving public awareness and education about its environmental work. The amount of information being provided has increased sharply. Publications on a wide range of environmental issues are available, and the bimonthly "Environment Bulletin" has built up a considerable circulation. The decision to make environment the subject of the 1992 *World Development Report* is also significant, since the document will be a distillation of all the Bank's analytical work in this area.

Future Directions

There continues to be a pressing need—in developing and industrial countries alike—to use increasingly scarce natural resources more efficiently. The means of so doing will depend on a vastly improved understanding of the long-term consequences and the underlying causes of environmental degradation. Increased effort will be needed to identify appropriate social, economic, and other policy measures for sound environmental management. Tracing through the chain of causality is important but often difficult—as the example of tropical deforestation shows very clearly. Environmental strategy work aimed at developing this understanding should be a prerequisite for structural and sector policy reform. This will require training, institutional strengthening, and the transfer of technologies that can help populations to adapt to changing natural resource endowments.

Improved understanding of the links between poverty and environment remains a priority. While the poor and disadvantaged tend to suffer most from environmental degradation and while poverty is an obstacle to bringing about environmental improvement, it is difficult to generalize about the extent to which poverty is itself responsible for environmental problems. Indeed, as noted in this report, some of the most pressing environmental problems facing the planet are those originating in the wealthy countries. During the past year some work was begun on analyzing the relationships between poverty and environmental degradation, with special attention to the extent to which these problems are compounded by population growth. More applied research is still required, however, to identify equitable environmental policies at both the national and international level.

Recent lessons from both environmental strategy work and project experience show that good economics is typically good for the environment. There are innumerable opportunities for investments and policy reforms that meet both environmental and economic objectives—and this fact is consistent with the growing evidence that environmental degradation is undermining sustainable development in many countries. However, there will always be important instances in which economic and environmental objectives conflict to some extent. For example, limits may exist to the environmental benefits that can be derived from trade liberalization. Clearly, market mechanisms, for all their advantages, will not cover the full environmental agenda unless they are supplemented by government interventions of various kinds. In particular, the role of "green taxes," possibly substituting for taxes on income or capital, should be carefully considered for developing countries. Improving the Bank's ability to advise governments in this area commands high priority in its future work program.

For the longer term the key question concerns the feasibility of continued economic growth on a global scale. Economic growth has traditionally been linked with the depletion of the earth's natural resources and is now placing growing pressure on the earth's assimilative capacity. In light of rapid rates of population growth, it is clear that prospects for future economic development depend heavily on technical progress in using resources efficiently. The Bank will continue to help the developing countries respond to this challenge in three ways:

- By providing assistance for projects and policies that meet both economic and environmental criteria
- By assisting in international efforts to mobilize resources to implement environmental projects when concessionary finance is required
- By continuing to give special emphasis to population activities.

The finite nature of the earth's natural resources and its assimilative capacity means that the Bank's efforts must be complemented and paralleled by an international effort, involving industrial countries as much as developing countries. Not only is there a growing economic interdependence among countries, but there is a growing physical interdependence as well, as exemplified by the "global commons" issues of greenhouse warming and threats to the ozone layer. The developing countries, assisted by external agencies such as the World Bank, can do much to improve the management of their environment, often in ways that are also consistent with the objective of economic growth. However, their efforts may be frustrated by policies and environmentally destructive activities beyond their control, such as those originating in the industrial countries. A partnership is needed that involves not only policy reform in the industrial countries, but also efforts to improve the scientific basis for decisionmaking, such as the prediction of the local and global environmental consequences of activities as well as scientific and technical research designed to adapt to or to avoid continued environmental degradation. Such a global partnership, in which all countries play their part, is essential if enduring gains are to be achieved.

Annex I. Illustrative List of Projects with Environmental Components or Objectives Approved in Fiscal 1990

This annex provides details on 40 of the 117 projects approved in fiscal 1990 that had environmental components. These projects cover countries from all four regions of the Bank: Africa, Asia, Latin American and the Caribbean, and Europe, Middle East, and North Africa. The list illustrates the range of environmental components included in Bank projects.

Country	Project	Environmental components
Bangladesh	Bangladesh Water Development Board Systems Rehabilitation	Improve the operation and maintenance of three large irrigation projects covering 60,000 hectares of irrigable land and of seven small flood control and drainage subprojects covering about 40,000 hectares to provide better drainage
	Fisheries III	Develop coastal shrimp culture by improving the infrastructure for public water control on 13,000 hectares already under shrimp culture; develop floodplain fisheries by stocking 29,000 hectares of major floodplains; develop other fisheries programs; provide institutional support
Bolivia	Eastern Lowlands Regional Development	Support the planning and management of natural resources by preparing a land-use plan for the region that encompasses the results of agroecological zoning, soil studies and mapping, and studies on water, forestry, livestock, and land tenure; protect forest reserves and national parks, such as Noel Kempf Mercado National Park; protect indigenous people; demarcate tribal lands.

Country	Project	Environmental components
Brazil	Electricity Transmission and Conservation Project	Implement energy conservation measures; provide training on how to apply energy conservation technology; carry out studies on cogeneration using residual biomass fuels; prepare environmental impact assessments related to constructing transmission works.
	Land Management II	Provide land use mapping, planning, and monitoring for 520 project microcatchments; develop an incentive program for land management, soil conservation, and pollution control to help farmers belonging to a microcatchment association properly plan land management and implement collective soil conservation and agricultural pollution control measures; plan erosion control works along rural roads to be implemented as integral parts of microcatchment management plans; support forestry development and protection of natural resources through forestry conservation programs; develop environmental legislation concerning land use, soil conservation, and agricultural pollution; support management of state parks and protection of biological reserves.
Burkina Faso	Urban II	Develop a solid waste management system and drainage improvements.
Burundi	Transport Sector	Provide technical assistance for developing institutional capacity to review and evaluate the potential environmental impacts of road works (such as risks of erosion, drainage problems, and compaction of earth roads) and to design appropriate remedies if needed; incorporate safeguards in bidding documents and contracts to minimize potential environmental damage caused by road works.
Cameroon	Agricultural Extension Training	Develop techniques to protect catchments and conserve soil; support adaptive research to develop pest- and disease-resistant crop varieties.

Country	Project	Environmental components
China	Jiangxi Agricultural Development	Establish 6,705 hectares of pine forestry; develop environmental design specifications and monitoring arrangements for the project's agroprocessing activities (such as feedmills) to ensure compliance with environmental standards; develop a program to educate farmers in pesticide use and proper methods of application.
	National Afforestation	Establish 985,000 hectares of forest plantations on hilly and barren lands; introduce environmental guidelines for forest plantations on issues such as soil conservation, pest control, and species diversity; prepare pilot plans for managing forest resources.
Colombia	Small-Scale Irrigation Project	Reforest about 750 hectares in water catchment areas for irrigation schemes; construct gully plugs, trenches, and terraces in about 325 hectares of critical watershed areas; provide environmental supervision of irrigation subprojects.
Guinea	Urban II	Rehabilitate urban infrastructure, such as paved roads and storm water drainage, to minimize dust pollution and limit flooding; coordinate with ongoing environmental action plan to develop coherent policies and national programs in various areas, including urban environment.
India	Industrial Technology Development	Support environmental protection activities, such as reducing pollution from tannery effluents; support laboratory and industrial safety through a system of interventions, such as a program for integrity evaluation that could help prevent major environmental disasters.
	Petrochemicals Development II	Require agreements to ensure that emissions of air pollutants, water effluents, and solid wastes comply with environmental guidelines.

Country	Project	Environmental components
India (*continued*)	Punjab Irrigation II	Line irrigation canals and water courses to improve irrigation efficiency and prevent waterlogging; provide drainage works in currently waterlogged areas and extensive pilot works in ground water drainage; provide Kandi Low Dams and catchment stabilization to protect downstream areas from flash floods.
	Watershed Plains and Hills Projects	Reverse degradation of the natural environment by conserving soil and moisture through techniques such as vegetative cover treatments; support innovative management system of common lands that would enhance the supply of fodder, fuelwood, and foodcrops without causing further environmental degradation.
Indonesia	Jabotabek Water and Sanitation Development	Develop a program of physical investments, technical assistance, and policies for managing water resources and water quality management through water and sewerage components, improved waste water disposal, and water resources management studies.
	Secondary Education II	Develop an environmental studies teaching program to be integrated into the existing science, social studies, and geography curriculum in secondary education.
Jordan	Integrated Phosphate Project	Design fertilizer plant to limit dust emissions, recover fine particles, and dispose of slimes and effluents.
Kenya	Coffee Improvement II	Install full water recirculation and pollution control systems in factories, which would entail separating coffee pulp and water, disposing of pulp, and recirculating process water.)
Korea, Republic of	Technology Advancement II	Provide technical assistance to the Korea Institute of Energy and Resources to explore ways to substitute existing energy sources with more efficient, less-polluting, and renewable resources.

Country	Project	Environmental components
Lao People's Democratic Republic	Upland Agricultural Development	Reverse environmental degradation on hillside slopes by using soil and water conservation technology; replace traditional slash-and-burn methods with cropping practices; research soil management packages, such as the use of tree crops, forestry, and inexpensive vegetative soil retention methods.
Mauritius	Highways II	Improve road safety and air quality through traffic management component and vehicle emission control.
Mexico	Forestry Durango and Chihuahua Project	Improve forest management and controlled forest utilization in previously harvested and degraded pine and oak forests; reforest areas incapable of productive natural regeneration; strengthen the administration of parks and reserves; finance research and protection of endangered species; strengthen the management and coordination capabilities of federal and state forestry and conservation institutions; implement an environmental monitoring program; train Indian ejidos and communities in forestry management and utilization; provide technical and legal assistance to Indian ejidos on land tenure and resource control issues.
Nepal	Groundwater Irrigation I	Prevent waterlogging; undertake environmental assessments of subprojects involving construction activities.
Niger	National Agricultural Research	Carry out applied research to develop improved land, water, crop, livestock, and forestry management practices.
Nigeria	Agricultural Development Projects	Help to develop state environmental action plans.

Country	Project	Environmental components
Nigeria (*continued*)	Oyo State Urban Project	Implement a pilot erosion control project in Ibadan's hilly zones; reclaim a 20-hectare refuse dump site; improve solid waste management, storm drainage, and flood control; establish an Environmental Management Department to develop statewide environmental policy and programs, establish and monitor standards, and undertake environmental improvement programs.
Pakistan	Agricultural Research II	Implement a program of integrated pest management; carry out studies on waterlogging and salinity; improve irrigation efficiency and drainage; improve the management of watersheds and rangelands.
Philippines	Energy Sector Loan	Prepare an environmental impact assessment for each energy subproject to cover problems such as emission of hydrogen sulfides, noise and thermal releases in geothermal fields, drainage of geothermal fluids, and pollutants from coal-fired power plants; improve environmental standards and monitoring; strengthen the institutional and technical capabilities of the Bureau of Environmental Management to carry out monitoring tasks.
	Industrial Investment Credit Project	Carry out subsector restructuring studies to review environmental standards and existing pollution control measures; develop more comprehensive studies of measures to improve environmental regulatory capacity and establish a mechanism to finance pollution control activities; request participating financial institutions to require that subprojects comply with Philippine environmental laws and regulations.

Country	Project	Environmental components
Philippines (*continued*)	Municipal Development Project II	Construct and rehabilitate drainage facilities, such as collector drains, canals, and pipes; provide technical assistance for a study on solid waste collection, disposal, and management.
Senegal	Agricultural Services	Improve cultural practices and herd management, through soil conservation, water harvesting, contour planting, zero tilling, composting, alley-cropping, and agroforestry.
Somalia	Farahaane Irrigation Rehabilitation	Develop and rehabilitate irrigation works; carry out studies on integrated pest management and land tenure; improve land titling.
Thailand	Second Power System Development Project	Implement measures to strengthen EGAT's capabilities in environmental monitoring and evaluation through a formal document stating its environmental policy and objectives; restructure its Environmental Division to organize functions according to the areas of general environmental management, atmospheric environmental issues, aquatic environmental issues, acoustic environmental issues, and social/resettlement issues; provide technical assistance and training in interpretive evaluation and qualitative prediction.
Turkey	Agricultural Extension II	Develop a program of integrated pest management, soil erosion control measures, and agroforestry.
	Ankara Sewerage Project	Expand sewage collection services to benefit 850,000 people; improve present sewerage services to about 500,000 people; construct drainage systems to reduce the risk of flooding.
Yemen, Republic of	Emergency Flood Reconstruction Project	Rehabilitate flood protection and irrigation structures; provide technical assistance for a flood preparedness and mitigation study.

Country	Project	Environmental components
Yemen, Republic of *(continued)*	National Agricultural Sector Management Project	Improve the management of irrigated agriculture; monitor and regulate the exploitation of water resources; support wildlife protection and the development of a Wildlife Conservation Directorate.
	Power III	Improve fuel use efficiency.

Annex II. Expenditures by Bank Environmental Units in Fiscal 1990

(thousands of dollars)

	Environment Department	Regional divisions				Total
		Africa	Asia	Europe, Middle East, and North Africa	Latin America and the Caribbean	
Bank funded						
Salary budget	1,692	444	627	601	498	3,862
Nonsalary budget	1,518	318	542	648	113	3,139
Research committee	109	–	–	–	–	109
Environmental Assessment Fund	–	1,088	700	588	185	2,561
Subtotal	3,319	1,850	1,869	1,837	796	9,671
Non-Bank funded[a]						
France	–	–	–	5	–	5
Japan	–	–	103	–	–	103
Norway	442	568	304	140	122	1,576
Sweden	–	–	–	45	–	45
United States	–	–	–	59	–	59
UNDP	183	–	–	28	–	28
Subtotal	625	568	407	277	122	1,999
Total	3,944	2,418	2,276	2,114	918	11,670

—Not applicable or negligible.
a. Includes where appropriate seconded staff.

Bibliography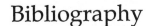

The following titles were formally published by the World Bank during fiscal 1990 and may be obtained from the bookstores at the Bank offices in Washington, D.C., and Paris or through the Bank's authorized commercial distributors and depository libraries throughout the world. University press books are available also from the presses named. An asterisk (*) indicates titles published before July 1989 but considered significant enough be mentioned in this first annual report.

*Ahmad, Yusuf J., Salah El Serafy, and Ernst Lutz, eds. 1989. *Environmental Accounting for Sustainable Development*. A UNEP-World Bank Symposium.

Anderson, Jock R., and Jesuthanson Thampapillai. 1990. *Soil Conservation in Developing Countries: Project and Policy Intervention*. Policy and Research Series 8.

Arrhenius, Erik, and Thomas W. Waltz. 1990. *The Greenhouse Effect: Implications for Economic Development*. World Bank Discussion Paper 78.

Dixon, John, Lee Talbot, and Guy Le Moigne. 1990. *Dams and the Environment: Considerations in World Bank Projects*. World Bank Technical Paper 110.

Gregersen, Hans, Sydney Draper, and Dieter Elz, eds. 1989. *People and Trees: The Role of Social Forestry in Sustainable Development*. Economic Development Institute Seminar Series.

Hicks, James, with Herman Daly, Shelton Davis, and Maria de Lourdes de Freitas. 1990. *Ecuador's Amazon Region*. World Bank Discussion Paper 75.

Kiss, A., and F. Meerman. Forthcoming. *Integrated Pest Management and African Agriculture*. World Bank Technical Paper.

Le Moigne, Guy, Shawki Barghouti, and Herve Plusquellec, editors. 1990. *Dam Safety and the Environment*. World Bank Technical Paper 115.

McNeely, Jeffrey A., Kenton R. Miller, Walter V. Reid, Russell A. Mittermeier, and Timothy B. Werner. 1990. *Conserving the World's Biological Diversity*. Joint publication of the World Bank, World Resources Institute, International Union for the Conservation of Nature and Natural Resources, Conservation International, and World Wildlife Fund-US.

✓ Schramm, Gunter, and Jeremy J. Warford, eds. 1989. *Environmental Management and Economic Development*. Baltimore, Md.: The Johns Hopkins University Press.

*World Bank. 1987. *Environment, Growth and Development*. Development Committee Pamphlet No. 14.

*————. 1988. *Environment and Development: Implementing the World Bank's New Policies*. Development Committee Pamphlet 17.

————. 1989a. *Philippines: Environment and Natural Resource Management Study*.

————. 1989b. *Renewable Resource Management in Agriculture*. An Operations Evaluation Study.

————. 1989c. *Sub-Saharan Africa: From Crisis to Sustainable Growth*. A Long-Term Perspective Study.

————. 1989d. *World Bank Support for the Environment: A Progress Report*. Development Committee Pamphlet 22.

————. 1990a. *Evaluation Results for 1988: Issues in World Bank Lending over Two Decades*. An Operations Evaluation Study.

————. 1990b. *Vetiver Grass: The Hedge against Erosion*.

————. 1990c. *World Development Report 1990*. New York: Oxford University Press.

World Bank and the European Investment Bank. 1990. *The Environmental Program for the Mediterranean: Preserving a Shared Heritage and Managing a Common Resource*.

The following titles were produced by various departments within the World Bank during fiscal 1990 and may be obtained by writing directly to the Environment Department.

Anderson, Mary B. 1990. "Analyzing the Costs and Benefits of Natural Disaster Responses in the Context of Development." Environment Department Working Paper 29.

Bartone, Carl R., Janis Bernstein, and Frederick Wright. 1990. "Investments in Solid Waste Management: Opportunities for Environmental Improvement." Policy, Research, and External Affairs Working Paper 405.

Bhattarcharya, Rina. 1990. "Common Property Externalities: Isolation, Assurance, and Resource Depletion in a Traditional Grazing Context." Environment Department, Policy and Research Division Working Paper 1990-10.

Bie, Stein. 1990. "Dryland Degradation Measurement Techniques." Environment Department Working Paper 26.

Bishop, Joshua, and Jennifer Allen. 1989. "The On-Site Costs of Soil Erosion in Mali." Environment Department Working Paper 21.

Butcher, D. 1990. "A Review of the Treatment of Environmental Aspects of Bank Energy Projects." Industry and Energy Department Paper 24.

Conable, Barber B. 1989. "Development and the Environment: A Global Balance." Remarks at the Conference on Global Environment and Human Response toward Sustainable Development, Tokyo, Japan.

Costanza, Robert, Ben Haskell, Laura Cornwell, Herman Daly, and Twig Johnson. 1990. "The Ecological Economics of Sustainability: Making Local and Short-Term

Goals Consistent with Global and Long-Term Goals." Environment Department Working Paper 32.

Dixon, John A., and Louise A. Fallon. 1989. "The Concept of Sustainability: Origins, Extensions, and Usefulness for Policy." Environment Department, Policy and Research Division Working Paper 1989-1.

✓ Foy, George, and Herman Daly. 1989. "Allocation, Distribution, and Scale as Determinants of Environmental Degradation: Case Studies of Haiti, El Salvador, and Costa Rica." Environment Department Working Paper 19.

Goodland, R. J. A. 1989. "Environment and Development: Progress of the World Bank (and Speculation towards Sustainability)." Environment Department, Policy and Research Division Working Paper 1989-5.

Hamrin, Robert D. 1990. "Policy Control Options for Comparative Air Pollution Study in Urban Areas." Environment Department Working Paper 28.

✓ Jagannathan, Vijay. 1989. "Poverty, Public Policies, and the Environment." Environment Department, Policy and Research Division Working Paper 24.

————. 1990. "Poverty-Environment Linkages: Case Study of West Java." Environment Department, Policy and Research Division Working Paper 1990-8.

Jagannathan, Vijay, Hideki Mori, and Hassan M. Hassan. 1990. "Applications of Geographical Information Systems in Economic Analysis: A Case Study of Uganda." Environment Department Working Paper 27.

Jagannathan, Vijay, and A. O. Ogunbiade. 1990. "Poverty Environment Linkages in Nigeria: Issues for Research." Environment Department Working Paper 1990-7.

Kiss, A. ed. Forthcoming. "Living with Wildlife: Wildlife Utilization with Local Participation in Africa."

Kosmo, Mark. 1989. "Economic Incentives and Industrial Pollution in Developing Countries." Environment Department, Policy and Research Division Working Paper 1989-2.

Kreimer, Alcira. 1989. "Reconstruction after Earthquakes: Sustainability and Development." Environment Department, Policy and Research Division Working Paper 1989-3.

Kreimer, Alcira, and Michele Zador, eds. 1989. "Colloquium on Disasters, Sustainability, and Development: A Look at the 1990s." Environment Department Working Paper 23.

Krupnick, Alan, and Adelaida Alicbusan. 1990. "Estimation of Health Benefits of Reduction in Ambient Air Pollutants." Environment Department, Policy and Research Division Working Paper 1990-11.

Krupnick, Alan, and Iona Sebastian. 1990. "Issues in Urban Air Pollution: Review of the Beijing Case." Environment Department Working Paper 31.

Lutz, Ernst, and Michael Young. 1990. "Agricultural Policies in Industrial Countries and Their Environmental Impacts: Applicability to and Comparisons with Developing Nations." Environment Department Working Paper 25.

MacKnight, Scott, and others. 1989. "The Environmentally Sound Disposal of Dredged Materials." Infrastructure and Urban Development Department Discussion Paper 54.

Magrath, William. 1989. "Economic Analysis of Soil Conservation Technologies." Environment Department, Policy and Research Division Working Paper 1989-4.

Magrath, William, and P. L. Arens. 1989. "The Costs of Soil Erosion on Java: A Natural Resource Accounting Approach." Environment Department Working Paper 18.

Magrath, William, and John B. Doolette. 1990. "Strategic Issues for Watershed Development in Asia." Environment Department Working Paper 30.

Mortimore, Michael. 1989. "The Causes, Nature, and Rate of Soil Degradation in the Northernmost States of Nigeria and An Assessment of the Role of Fertilizer in Counteracting the Processes of Degradation." Environment Department Working Paper 17.

Rasmussen, Jens, and Roger Batstone. 1989. "Why Do Complex Organizational Systems Fail?" Environment Department Working Paper 20.

Sebastian, Iona, and Adelaida Alicbusan. 1989. "Sustainable Development: Issues in Adjustment Lending Policies." Environment Department, Policy and Research Division Working Paper 1989-6.

Seve, Juan E., Bruce A. Ross-Sheriff, Peter C. Impara, Diana de Treville. 1990. "World Bank Drylands Management Study: Lessons of Experience." Environment Department, Policy and Research Division Working Paper 1990-9.

Sinha, Jumaries, Amiy Varma, James Souba, and Asif Faiz. 1989. "Environmental and Ecological Considerations in Land Transport: A Resource Guide." Infrastructure and Urban Development Department Discussion Paper 41.

Trolldalen, Jon-Martin. 1990. "Professional Development Workshop on Dryland Management." Environment Department Working Paper 33.

Wells, Michael, Katrina Brandon, and Lee Hannah. Forthcoming. "People and Parks: Linking Protected Area Management with Local Communities." Jointly prepared by the World Bank, World Wildlife Fund, and US Agency for International Development.

World Bank. 1989a. "Emergency Recovery Assistance. Operational Directive 8.50.

———. 1989b. "Environmental Assessment." Operational Directive 4.00, Annex A.

———. 1989c. "Environmental Policy for Dam and Reservoir Projects." Operational Directive 4.00, Annex B.

———. 1990. "Involuntary Resettlement." Operational Directive 4.30.

World Bank and the United Nations Development Programme. 1989. "Energy Sector Management Assistance Program Annual Report."